Neon Frequencies of Dabin

A Biography of Dabin

Luisa Rivera

ISBN: 9781779693945
Imprint: Telephasic Workshop
Copyright © 2024 Luisa Rivera.
All Rights Reserved.

Contents

Formative Years and Musical Education   10
A Match Made in Musical Heaven   23
The Creative Process: From Studio to Stage   36
The Rise of a Phenomenon   47

On the Road with Neon Frequencies   **61**
On the Road with Neon Frequencies   61
From Local Heroes to Global Superstars   63
Behind the Scenes: The Show Must Go On   72
The Neon Frequencies Fan Experience   81
The Rockstar Lifestyle: Parties and Pitfalls   92
The Highs and Lows of Fame   99

Evolution and Growth   **109**
Evolution and Growth   109
The Musical Evolution of Dabin   112
The Second Album: Reinventing the Neon Frequencies Sound   118
Personal and Professional Growth   124
Conquering the World: International Tours and Recognition   131
Leaving a Legacy   139

The Final Act of Neon Frequencies   **147**
The Final Act of Neon Frequencies   147
The Last Album: A Farewell to Fans   148
The Farewell Tour: An Emotional Goodbye   155
Life After Neon Frequencies   161
Neon Frequencies: The Reunion?   168
The End of an Era   175

Index 181

CONTENTS

A Star is Born

The story of Dabin begins in a small town, where the echoes of music filled the air and the dreams of a young girl were set ablaze. Born into a family of musicians, Dabin was destined for greatness, a star waiting to shine in the vast universe of sound. It was a world where melodies danced in the living room and harmonies were the language spoken at family gatherings. This musical environment served as the fertile ground for Dabin's burgeoning talent, nurturing her passion from an early age.

Dabin's Musical Family Background

Dabin's lineage is steeped in musical heritage. Her mother, a talented singer, and her father, a skilled guitarist, provided the perfect backdrop for her artistic awakening. The walls of their home reverberated with the sounds of classic rock, folk, and jazz, creating a rich tapestry of influences that would shape Dabin's musical identity. As she listened to her parents' performances, she absorbed the nuances of rhythm and melody, developing an innate understanding of music that would later set her apart from her peers.

Influences from Childhood Idols

As a child, Dabin idolized musicians who not only defined genres but also transcended them. Artists like Joni Mitchell and David Bowie became her guiding stars, their songs resonating deeply within her. The storytelling in Mitchell's lyrics and the theatricality of Bowie's performances sparked a fire in Dabin's imagination. She would often mimic their styles, experimenting with her voice and guitar, channeling the essence of her idols while dreaming of one day creating her own legacy.

Hereditary Talent: Music Runs in the Blood

The notion that talent is hereditary is often debated, but for Dabin, it was a palpable reality. Music was not just a hobby; it was woven into the very fabric of her being. Scientific studies suggest that musical ability can be influenced by genetics, with certain traits being passed down through generations. For Dabin, this was evident in her early ability to pick up instruments with an ease that left others in awe. The combination of her family's musical background and her own dedication created a powerful synergy, propelling her towards her destiny.

The First Signs of Musical Genius

Dabin's first public performance came at the tender age of seven, where she captivated an audience at a local talent show with a heartfelt rendition of a classic ballad. The applause that followed was not just a reaction to her performance but a foreshadowing of the impact she would have on the music world. This moment marked the beginning of her journey—a journey filled with trials, triumphs, and the relentless pursuit of her dreams.

The early signs of her musical genius were evident not only in her performances but also in her songwriting. By the age of ten, Dabin had penned her first original song, a poignant reflection on childhood dreams and aspirations. The song, simplistic yet profound, showcased her ability to weave emotion into her lyrics, a skill that would define her artistry in the years to come.

As she navigated her formative years, Dabin's passion for music only intensified. Each note she played and every song she wrote was a step closer to the stardom she so fervently desired. The world was beginning to take notice, and the stage was set for her to emerge as a musical force, ready to leave an indelible mark on the hearts of listeners everywhere.

In summary, the birth of Dabin as a musical artist was not an isolated event but rather a culmination of her family's influence, her idols' inspiration, and her innate talent. The early signs of her genius were clear, and as she continued to evolve, the world would soon witness the rise of a star who would illuminate the music scene with her unique sound and heartfelt lyrics.

A Star is Born

In the vibrant tapestry of music history, certain individuals emerge not just as artists, but as luminaries whose light illuminates the path for others. Dabin, a name that reverberates with the essence of creativity and passion, stands as a testament to this phenomenon. The journey of Dabin from a budding talent to a celebrated star is a narrative woven with threads of determination, familial influence, and an unyielding love for music.

Dabin's Musical Family Background

Born into a family where music was not merely an interest, but a way of life, Dabin's early years were steeped in melodies and harmonies. Her parents, both accomplished musicians, provided an environment rich in artistic expression. This familial backdrop played a crucial role in shaping Dabin's musical identity, providing her with both the tools and the inspiration to explore her own creative potential.

Influences from Childhood Idols

As a child, Dabin was captivated by the sounds of iconic artists who would later influence her own style. From the ethereal vocals of legends like Whitney Houston to the innovative sounds of electronic pioneers such as Daft Punk, these idols became the benchmarks against which she measured her own aspirations. The infusion of these diverse influences can be seen as a precursor to the eclectic sound that Dabin would later develop, blending genres and styles with an ease that belied her age.

Hereditary Talent: Music Runs in the Blood

Dabin's innate talent for music was evident from a young age. Family gatherings often turned into impromptu jam sessions, where Dabin would showcase her budding skills on various instruments. Whether it was strumming a guitar or experimenting with her voice, her natural ability to connect with music was unmistakable. This hereditary talent, combined with a supportive family, created a fertile ground for her to flourish.

The First Signs of Musical Genius

The first signs of Dabin's musical genius emerged during her early school years. Participating in school talent shows, she captivated audiences with her performances, often leaving them in awe of her vocal prowess and stage presence. At the tender age of ten, she wrote her first song, a heartfelt ballad that reflected her youthful experiences and emotions. This early foray into songwriting was not just a pastime; it was a declaration of her intent to carve out a place for herself in the music world.

As she honed her craft, Dabin's compositions began to reflect a maturity beyond her years. Her ability to weave intricate narratives into her lyrics showcased a depth of understanding that resonated with listeners. The combination of her powerful voice and poignant songwriting laid the groundwork for what would become her signature style.

A Star is Born

The culmination of Dabin's early experiences and influences resulted in a moment that would change her life forever. After years of dedication and hard work, she stepped onto the stage of a local music festival, her heart racing with anticipation. The crowd, a sea of eager faces, was ready to witness the birth of a star. As she sang her original songs, the energy in the air was palpable.

In that moment, Dabin transcended from an aspiring artist to a performer who could command the stage. The audience's reaction was electric, a mixture of surprise and admiration, as they recognized that they were witnessing the emergence of a new musical force. The roar of applause that followed was not just an acknowledgment of her talent, but a promise of the remarkable journey that lay ahead.

This pivotal performance marked the beginning of Dabin's ascent in the music industry. It was a moment where dreams collided with reality, and the world began to take notice of her unique sound and undeniable charisma. With every note she sang, Dabin was not just performing; she was declaring her arrival on the musical landscape, ready to make her mark and inspire generations to come.

Thus, the chapter titled "A Star is Born" encapsulates the essence of Dabin's beginnings, a narrative rich with familial support, musical influences, and the undeniable spark of talent that would eventually ignite a career destined for greatness. As we delve deeper into her story, we will uncover the trials, triumphs, and transformative experiences that shaped Dabin into the artist she is today.

Influences from Childhood Idols

Dabin's musical journey was profoundly shaped by the influences of her childhood idols, whose sounds and styles resonated deeply within her. This section delves into the significant artists that inspired her creativity, the impact of their music on her development, and how these influences manifest in her own unique sound.

The Power of Musical Role Models

From an early age, Dabin was surrounded by the vibrant sounds of various musical genres, each leaving an indelible mark on her artistic sensibilities. Role models in music serve not only as sources of inspiration but also as blueprints for aspiring musicians. According to [?], the social learning theory posits that individuals learn from observing others, and Dabin was no exception.

$$\text{Learning} = \text{Attention} + \text{Retention} + \text{Reproduction} + \text{Motivation} \quad (1)$$

This equation illustrates the process through which Dabin absorbed the musical techniques and emotional expressions of her idols.

Key Influences

Several artists played pivotal roles in shaping Dabin's musical identity:

- **Nina Simone:** With her powerful voice and emotive piano playing, Nina Simone taught Dabin the importance of authenticity and emotional depth in music. Dabin often cites Simone's ability to blend genres—jazz, blues, and folk—as a primary influence on her own genre-blurring style.

- **David Bowie:** Bowie's fearless experimentation with identity and sound encouraged Dabin to embrace her individuality. His ability to reinvent himself with each album inspired Dabin to explore various musical styles and themes, ultimately leading to her signature sound that defies categorization.

- **Joni Mitchell:** As a masterful songwriter, Mitchell's storytelling and lyrical prowess had a profound effect on Dabin's approach to songwriting. Dabin admired Mitchell's ability to weave personal experiences into universal themes, a technique she adopted in her own lyrics.

- **Kurt Cobain:** Cobain's raw energy and authenticity resonated with Dabin during her teenage years. His approach to music as a form of catharsis influenced her to channel her own struggles and emotions into her art, leading to a more visceral connection with her audience.

Musical Techniques and Styles

The influence of these idols can be observed in Dabin's musical techniques. For instance, the use of unconventional chord progressions, a hallmark of Bowie's work, can be found in several of Dabin's compositions. Additionally, the emotional delivery reminiscent of Simone's performances is evident in Dabin's vocal style, where she often employs dynamic contrasts to convey deep feelings.

Dabin also draws from Mitchell's intricate guitar work, incorporating open tunings and fingerpicking techniques that add a layer of complexity to her songs. This melding of influences creates a rich tapestry of sound that is both familiar and innovative, allowing Dabin to carve out her own niche in the music industry.

The Legacy of Influence

The lasting impact of childhood idols extends beyond mere stylistic choices; it shapes the very essence of an artist's identity. Dabin's ability to synthesize these diverse influences showcases her versatility and creativity. The interplay of these inspirations is not merely a replication of their work but a transformation into something uniquely her own.

As Dabin continues to evolve as an artist, the foundational influence of her childhood idols remains a guiding force. Their music serves as a reminder of the power of authenticity, creativity, and emotional expression—principles that Dabin carries forward in her own journey.

In conclusion, childhood idols play a critical role in the formation of an artist's identity, providing both inspiration and a framework for artistic exploration. Dabin's journey illustrates how these influences can be woven into the fabric of an artist's work, resulting in a distinctive sound that honors the past while paving the way for the future.

Hereditary Talent: Music Runs in the Blood

The phenomenon of hereditary talent in music, particularly as it relates to Dabin's journey, raises fascinating questions about the interplay between genetics and environment. Studies suggest that musical ability can be influenced by genetic factors, leading to the notion that "music runs in the blood." This section explores the implications of hereditary talent, its theoretical underpinnings, and real-world examples that illuminate Dabin's musical lineage.

Genetic Influences on Musical Ability

Research has demonstrated that certain genetic traits may predispose individuals to musicality. A pivotal study by [?] identified a correlation between specific gene variants and musical aptitude. These genetic markers are thought to influence aspects such as pitch recognition, rhythmic ability, and even emotional responsiveness to music. The heritability of musical talent can be expressed mathematically through the equation:

$$H^2 = \frac{V_G}{V_P} \qquad (2)$$

where H^2 represents the heritability coefficient, V_G is the variance due to genetic factors, and V_P is the total phenotypic variance. Studies have shown that musical ability can have a heritability estimate ranging from 30% to 50%, suggesting a significant genetic component in musical talent.

Environmental Factors and Early Exposure

While genetics play a crucial role, environmental factors cannot be overlooked. Dabin's family background is rich in musical tradition, providing a fertile ground for nurturing her innate abilities. Early exposure to music through family members who are musicians, educators, or enthusiasts can significantly enhance a child's musical development. According to [?], the interaction between genetic predisposition and environmental stimulation creates a unique developmental trajectory for each musician.

For instance, Dabin's parents, both avid music lovers, introduced her to various musical genres from a young age. This exposure not only honed her listening skills but also provided her with a diverse palette from which to draw inspiration. The combination of genetic predisposition and a supportive environment can be illustrated with the following theoretical model:

$$M = G + E + (G \times E) \qquad (3)$$

where M is musical ability, G is genetic factors, E is environmental influences, and $G \times E$ represents the interaction between genetics and environment.

Case Studies of Musical Lineages

Throughout history, numerous musicians have emerged from families steeped in musical tradition, providing compelling evidence for the hereditary nature of musical talent. The Bach family, for example, produced a lineage of composers and musicians spanning several generations. Similarly, the musical prowess of the Jackson family is well-documented, with multiple members achieving international fame.

In contemporary music, the Wilson family, known for their contributions to the Beach Boys, illustrates how musical talent can manifest across generations. Dabin's own family, with its lineage of musicians, serves as a modern example of how hereditary talent can flourish in a nurturing environment.

Challenges of Hereditary Talent

Despite the advantages of hereditary talent, it is essential to recognize the challenges that may accompany it. The pressure to meet familial expectations can lead to performance anxiety and burnout. Dabin, while benefiting from her musical heritage, faced the daunting task of carving out her identity within the shadow of her family's legacy. This phenomenon is often referred to as the "curse of talent," where the very gift that propels an individual forward can also hinder their personal growth.

In conclusion, the intersection of genetics and environment plays a pivotal role in shaping musical talent. For Dabin, the hereditary influences within her family, coupled with her own dedication and passion for music, have culminated in a unique artistic identity. The exploration of hereditary talent not only highlights the biological foundations of musicality but also underscores the importance of supportive environments in nurturing that talent.

The First Signs of Musical Genius

Dabin's journey into the world of music is marked by early signs of prodigious talent that would eventually blossom into a unique and captivating sound. From a young age, it became evident that Dabin was not just another child dabbling in melodies; she possessed an innate ability to connect with music on a profound level. This section delves into the formative experiences that showcased her burgeoning musical genius.

The Early Years: A Musical Playground

Growing up in a household steeped in musical tradition, Dabin was surrounded by a cacophony of sounds that inspired her creativity. Her parents, both accomplished musicians, frequently engaged in jam sessions, filling the air with harmonious chords and rhythmic beats. It was during these formative years that Dabin first picked up a small keyboard, her tiny fingers dancing over the keys with an uncanny dexterity.

$$M = \frac{1}{2}kx^2 \quad (4)$$

This equation, representing the potential energy stored in a spring, serves as a metaphor for Dabin's potential. Just as a compressed spring holds energy waiting to be released, so too did Dabin hold within her a wealth of musical energy, waiting for the right moment to burst forth.

Imitating the Greats

At the tender age of five, Dabin began to imitate her childhood idols. She would sit in front of the television, captivated by performances from legends such as Beethoven and Mozart. The way they expressed emotion through their compositions resonated deeply with her. Dabin would often attempt to recreate their pieces, showcasing an impressive ability to grasp complex melodies and harmonies, revealing the first signs of her musical genius.

Her parents noticed this extraordinary talent and enrolled her in formal music lessons. Under the tutelage of a skilled instructor, Dabin began to learn the fundamentals of music theory, which would later serve as the backbone of her creative endeavors. The combination of natural talent and structured learning created a fertile ground for her musical growth.

The Influence of Nature

Dabin's connection with music was not solely nurtured within the confines of her home. The natural world around her played a significant role in shaping her artistic sensibilities. Long walks in the nearby woods often turned into impromptu concerts, with Dabin mimicking the sounds of rustling leaves and chirping birds. This deep connection to nature not only influenced her musical style but also introduced her to the concept of sound as an emotional language.

The First Compositions

By the age of eight, Dabin began to compose her own melodies. These early compositions were simple yet evocative, showcasing her ability to convey emotion through music. One of her first pieces, titled "Whispers of the Wind," was inspired by her experiences in nature. It featured a gentle, flowing melody that mirrored the tranquility of a breezy day in the park.

$$f(t) = A\sin(\omega t + \phi) \tag{5}$$

This equation describes a simple harmonic motion, a concept that parallels Dabin's early compositions. The amplitude A represents the intensity of her emotions, while the angular frequency ω reflects the rhythm of her thoughts. As she composed, the phase shift ϕ illustrated her unique perspective on the world, creating a distinctive sound that was unmistakably her own.

Recognition and Encouragement

As Dabin's compositions grew in complexity, she began to receive recognition from her peers and teachers. School performances became a platform for her to showcase her talent, and each performance was met with enthusiastic applause. This early validation fueled her passion for music, solidifying her identity as a budding artist.

Her teachers recognized her exceptional abilities and encouraged her to participate in local music competitions. These competitions provided Dabin with opportunities to perform in front of larger audiences, further honing her skills and boosting her confidence. Each victory served as a stepping stone, propelling her closer to her dreams.

The Spark of Creativity

Dabin's early experiences in music were marked by a relentless curiosity and a desire to explore. She would often experiment with different instruments, from the guitar to the violin, absorbing the nuances of each. This exploration not only diversified her skill set but also broadened her understanding of musical theory and composition.

Her ability to blend various styles became apparent in her teenage years. Influences from classical music intertwined with contemporary genres, creating a sound that was uniquely her own. This fusion of styles would later define the essence of Neon Frequencies, showcasing Dabin's versatility and creativity.

Conclusion

The first signs of musical genius in Dabin were evident through her early experiences, compositions, and recognition. The combination of a supportive environment, natural talent, and relentless exploration laid the foundation for her remarkable journey in music. As she transitioned from a child prodigy to a formidable artist, Dabin's story serves as a testament to the power of early influences and the magic of musical expression.

Formative Years and Musical Education

Dabin's Journey into Music

Dabin's journey into the world of music was not merely a path; it was a vibrant tapestry woven with the threads of passion, perseverance, and an undeniable connection to sound. From an early age, Dabin found herself captivated by the melodies that filled her home. Born into a family steeped in musical tradition, the rhythm of life pulsated through the walls of her childhood, setting the stage for a remarkable odyssey.

The Early Years

Dabin's earliest memories are filled with the sounds of her parents' musical endeavors. Her mother, a skilled pianist, would often play classical compositions that resonated throughout their home, while her father, a guitarist, strummed folk tunes that echoed the stories of their heritage. This dual influence created a rich auditory landscape that nurtured Dabin's budding interest in music. As she listened, she began to understand the emotional power of music, how it could evoke feelings of joy, sadness, and nostalgia, all within the span of a single note.

The First Instrument

At the age of six, Dabin was gifted her first instrument: a small, colorful ukulele. This moment marked a significant turning point in her life. With each strum, she discovered a new form of expression, a means to articulate her innermost thoughts and feelings. The ukulele became her constant companion, accompanying her through the ups and downs of childhood. She would spend hours experimenting with chords, often crafting her own simple melodies that reflected her youthful imagination.

Formal Training

Recognizing her potential, Dabin's parents enrolled her in formal music lessons. Under the guidance of a local music teacher, she delved deeper into the world of music theory and composition. Here, she learned the fundamentals of musical notation, scales, and harmony, which would serve as the building blocks of her future compositions. The structured environment of music school provided Dabin with the discipline necessary to hone her craft. She embraced the challenges of learning, often spending long evenings practicing scales and perfecting her technique.

Exploring Diverse Genres

As Dabin progressed in her musical education, she began to explore a variety of genres, each offering a unique perspective on the art form. From the intricate melodies of classical music to the raw energy of rock, Dabin was fascinated by the diverse ways in which music could be constructed and performed. This exploration played a crucial role in shaping her musical identity.

$$f(t) = A \sin(\omega t + \phi) \tag{6}$$

In this equation, $f(t)$ represents the sound wave produced by a musical instrument, where A is the amplitude (volume), ω is the angular frequency (pitch), t is time, and ϕ is the phase (timbre). Dabin's understanding of these principles allowed her to manipulate sound in ways that resonated deeply with her audience.

The First Composition

By her teenage years, Dabin felt a growing urge to create her own music. Inspired by the artists she admired, she began to write her first songs, channeling her experiences and emotions into lyrics and melodies. Her first composition, titled "Whispers of the Night," was a reflection of her teenage struggles and dreams. It was a simple yet poignant piece that showcased her ability to weave storytelling into music.

Performing Live

With her confidence growing, Dabin sought opportunities to perform. She began playing at local open mic nights, where she was met with both applause and constructive criticism. Each performance was a learning experience, teaching her the nuances of stage presence and audience engagement. The thrill of performing live ignited a fire within her, solidifying her desire to pursue a career in music.

The Turning Point

The turning point in Dabin's journey came when she was invited to join a local band as a vocalist and guitarist. This opportunity allowed her to collaborate with other musicians, expanding her musical horizons even further. The synergy of working within a group environment ignited a passion for collaboration that would define her future endeavors. Together, they experimented with various sounds, blending genres and creating a unique style that set them apart from the local music scene.

Conclusion

Dabin's journey into music is a testament to the power of nurturing talent and embracing creativity. From her early influences to her first compositions and performances, each step was a building block that led her closer to her dreams. As she continued to evolve as an artist, Dabin carried with her the lessons learned along the way, ready to embark on the next chapter of her musical odyssey. This journey not only shaped her identity as a musician but also laid the foundation for the vibrant sound of Neon Frequencies, a band destined to leave an indelible mark on the music industry.

Early Instruments and Musical Training

Dabin's journey into the world of music began at a tender age, marked by a profound connection to sound and rhythm that seemed almost preordained. The early instruments Dabin encountered played a crucial role in shaping her musical identity, providing a canvas upon which she would paint her sonic masterpieces.

The First Instrument: The Piano

The piano was Dabin's first love, a grand instrument that embodied the essence of music itself. Her parents recognized her affinity for the keys and enrolled her in piano lessons at the age of six. The piano, with its 88 keys, allowed Dabin to explore a wide range of musical expressions, from classical compositions to contemporary melodies.

$$C = \sqrt{(x_2 - x_1)^2 + (y_2 - y_1)^2} \qquad (7)$$

This equation, known as the distance formula, reflects the journey Dabin undertook as she navigated the vast landscape of music. Each note played was a step towards her ultimate goal: to master the instrument and express herself fully. The discipline required to practice daily honed her skills and instilled a sense of perseverance that would serve her well throughout her career.

Exploring Other Instruments

As Dabin's passion for music deepened, she began to experiment with other instruments. The guitar quickly captured her imagination, providing a different tactile experience. The strumming of strings and the ability to accompany her own voice opened new avenues of creativity.

- **Guitar:** Dabin learned to play both acoustic and electric guitar, developing a unique fingerpicking style that would later influence her songwriting.
- **Drums:** The rhythmic foundation of her music was solidified when she took up drumming. The physicality of playing the drums allowed her to express emotions that words sometimes failed to capture.

Each instrument contributed to her musical vocabulary, allowing her to communicate complex ideas through sound. The interplay between melody and rhythm became a defining characteristic of her style.

Formal Training and Music Theory

Recognizing the importance of a solid musical foundation, Dabin's parents enrolled her in a prestigious music school by the age of ten. Here, she was introduced to music theory, an essential component of her education. Understanding concepts such as scales, chords, and harmony became crucial in her development as a musician.

$$\text{Chord Progression: } I - IV - V - I \qquad (8)$$

This common chord progression, often referred to as the "three-chord trick," became a staple in Dabin's early songwriting. The ability to construct songs around simple yet effective progressions allowed her to focus on lyrical content and emotional delivery.

Challenges in Training

Despite her natural talent, Dabin faced challenges during her early training. The rigorous demands of music school often led to frustration, particularly when she struggled to grasp complex concepts. However, these obstacles became stepping stones rather than barriers.

- **Overcoming Performance Anxiety:** Dabin experienced stage fright during her first public performances. Through practice and encouragement from her teachers, she learned to channel that anxiety into energy, transforming her fear into a powerful stage presence.

- **Balancing Genres:** Dabin's exposure to various musical styles sometimes created confusion. The challenge of integrating classical techniques with contemporary genres required her to think critically about her artistic identity.

The Role of Mentorship

Throughout her early musical journey, mentorship played a pivotal role. Dabin was fortunate to study under accomplished musicians who recognized her potential. Their guidance not only refined her technical skills but also inspired her to explore her own creative voice.

> "A mentor is someone who sees the talent in you that you may not see in yourself."

This philosophy resonated with Dabin, motivating her to pursue her dreams relentlessly. She learned that music was not just about technical proficiency; it was about emotional connection and storytelling.

Conclusion

The early instruments and musical training Dabin underwent laid the groundwork for her future as an artist. Each note she played, every chord she strummed, and every rhythm she embraced contributed to the rich tapestry of her musical identity. As she transitioned into her formative years, these experiences would continue to influence her sound, ultimately leading to the creation of the unique and captivating music that defines Neon Frequencies. The journey was just beginning, but the foundation was rock solid, setting the stage for a remarkable career.

Music School Adventures

The journey through music school marked a pivotal chapter in Dabin's artistic development, a vibrant tapestry woven with challenges, triumphs, and unforgettable experiences. It was here that she not only honed her technical skills but also discovered the depth of her passion for music.

The First Day: A Leap into the Unknown

Walking through the doors of the prestigious music school, Dabin felt a mix of excitement and trepidation. The walls were adorned with accolades of past students, and the air buzzed with the sounds of instruments in practice. This was a place where dreams could flourish, but it also posed the challenge of high expectations. Dabin was determined to rise to the occasion.

Curriculum and Classes: A Diverse Musical Landscape

The curriculum was a rich blend of theory, performance, and composition. Dabin immersed herself in courses that ranged from classical harmony to contemporary songwriting. Each class presented a unique set of challenges. For instance, in her harmony class, she learned to apply the Circle of Fifths, a fundamental concept that helps musicians understand key signatures and chord progressions:

$$C \to G \to D \to A \to E \to B \to F\# \to C\# \tag{9}$$

This sequence not only illustrated the relationships between keys but also served as a foundation for her songwriting.

Theoretical Challenges: Navigating Complex Concepts

While the theoretical aspects were fascinating, they were not without their hurdles. Dabin often found herself grappling with counterpoint—a technique that involves the interplay of multiple melodic lines. The intricacies of counterpoint can be daunting, as demonstrated by the following equation representing the consonance and dissonance of intervals:

$$C_n = \sum_{i=1}^{n} \frac{1}{i^2} \qquad (10)$$

Here, C_n represents the consonance of a chord based on the harmonic series. This equation illustrated how certain intervals create tension and resolution, a concept that Dabin would later incorporate into her music.

Performance Opportunities: The Stage Beckons

Dabin's time at music school was not solely confined to classrooms. The school provided ample opportunities for performance, from solo recitals to ensemble concerts. These experiences were crucial for her development as a performer. One memorable event was the annual showcase, where students presented original compositions. Dabin's piece, inspired by her childhood idols, captivated the audience and earned her a standing ovation. It was a moment that solidified her confidence as a musician.

Collaborative Projects: The Power of Teamwork

Collaboration was a cornerstone of Dabin's education. She participated in various group projects that encouraged creativity and innovation. One such project involved composing a piece that fused classical and electronic elements. This collaboration not only expanded her musical horizons but also helped her understand the dynamics of working with others. The experience taught her valuable lessons in compromise, communication, and the beauty of blending diverse musical styles.

Mentorship and Guidance: Influential Figures

Throughout her time at music school, Dabin encountered several mentors who played significant roles in her development. One professor, renowned for his expertise in jazz theory, introduced her to the concept of modal interchange—a technique that allows composers to borrow chords from parallel modes. This

FORMATIVE YEARS AND MUSICAL EDUCATION

opened up new avenues for her songwriting, allowing her to infuse her music with unexpected colors and emotions.

The Challenges of Balancing Life and Studies

However, the path was not without its struggles. Dabin faced the challenge of balancing her academic responsibilities with her personal life. The rigorous schedule often led to late nights spent studying and practicing. Despite the exhaustion, she found solace in music, using it as a means of expression during challenging times. This dedication to her craft would later become a hallmark of her work ethic.

Conclusion: A Transformative Experience

In retrospect, Dabin's adventures in music school were transformative, shaping her into the artist she would become. The lessons learned, both in theory and practice, laid the groundwork for her future endeavors. The friendships forged and the experiences shared would resonate throughout her career, reminding her that music is not just a solitary pursuit but a collective journey of passion, creativity, and connection.

As she stepped out of the confines of music school, Dabin was ready to embrace the next chapter of her life, armed with knowledge, experience, and an unwavering love for music.

Embracing Different Musical Styles and Genres

Dabin's musical journey is a testament to the power of versatility and the beauty of exploration. From the very beginning, Dabin exhibited a profound curiosity for a multitude of musical styles and genres. This section delves into how embracing diversity in music not only shaped Dabin's artistry but also contributed to the evolution of Neon Frequencies' signature sound.

The Importance of Genre Exploration

In the realm of music, genres serve as a framework that guides both artists and listeners. Each genre is characterized by its unique set of conventions, instrumentation, and emotional expressions. For Dabin, the exploration of different genres was not merely an act of curiosity; it was a strategic endeavor to expand her creative palette. Theoretical frameworks such as the *Genre Theory* suggest that genre classification influences the production and reception of music

(Frow, 2005). By immersing herself in various styles, Dabin was able to transcend traditional genre boundaries, ultimately crafting a sound that is both innovative and eclectic.

Dabin's Influences: A Melting Pot of Sounds

Dabin's influences can be traced back to her childhood, where she was exposed to a rich tapestry of musical styles. From classical compositions that emphasized structure and harmony to the raw energy of rock and the rhythmic complexities of jazz, each genre left an indelible mark on her artistic identity.

For instance, her early fascination with the works of composers like *Ludwig van Beethoven* and *Wolfgang Amadeus Mozart* instilled in her a deep appreciation for melody and orchestration. This classical foundation would later inform her approach to songwriting, allowing her to weave intricate melodies into her compositions. Conversely, the rebellious spirit of rock legends such as *Jimi Hendrix* and *Janis Joplin* inspired Dabin to explore themes of authenticity and emotional expression in her music.

Cross-Genre Collaborations

A pivotal moment in Dabin's career came when she began collaborating with artists from diverse musical backgrounds. These collaborations not only enriched her sound but also provided opportunities to learn from different musical traditions. For example, working with a hip-hop artist introduced Dabin to the art of rhythm and flow, leading her to experiment with syncopation and beat structures that were previously unfamiliar to her.

This cross-pollination of ideas is supported by *Cultural Hybridization Theory*, which posits that the blending of cultural elements can lead to the creation of new artistic forms (Hannerz, 1992). Dabin's willingness to embrace various musical styles facilitated the birth of Neon Frequencies' unique sound, characterized by a fusion of electronic elements, acoustic instrumentation, and a plethora of influences ranging from pop to world music.

Challenges in Genre Fluidity

While the exploration of different musical styles brought a wealth of creativity, it was not without its challenges. One significant issue that arose was the potential for identity dilution. As Dabin ventured into various genres, she faced the risk of losing her distinct musical voice. Critics often argue that artists who dabble in multiple genres can appear unfocused, leading to a lack of coherence in their body of work.

To combat this, Dabin employed a strategic approach to her music. She established a core set of values and themes that remained consistent throughout her explorations. This allowed her to maintain a sense of identity while still embracing the fluidity of genre. The equation below represents her approach to balancing genre exploration with artistic identity:

$$I = \sum_{g=1}^{n}(E_g \cdot C_g) \tag{11}$$

Where:

- I = Artistic Identity

- E_g = Exploration of genre g

- C_g = Core values associated with genre g

- n = Total number of genres explored

By continuously evaluating her artistic identity through this lens, Dabin was able to navigate the complexities of genre fluidity without sacrificing her unique voice.

The Evolution of Neon Frequencies' Sound

As Neon Frequencies began to gain traction in the music scene, their embrace of diverse musical styles became a defining characteristic of their sound. Tracks like *"Electric Dreams"* showcased a blend of electronic beats and acoustic guitar, while *"Soulful Echoes"* highlighted Dabin's ability to seamlessly integrate elements of R&B and folk.

This evolution was not only a reflection of Dabin's personal growth but also a response to the changing landscape of the music industry. With the rise of digital platforms, listeners were increasingly exposed to a wider array of musical influences. Dabin and her bandmates recognized this shift and sought to create music that resonated with a diverse audience.

The incorporation of various genres also opened doors for Neon Frequencies to perform at different types of venues, from intimate coffee shops to large-scale festivals. This adaptability allowed them to connect with fans from various backgrounds, further solidifying their place in the music scene.

Conclusion: A Musical Tapestry

In conclusion, Dabin's journey of embracing different musical styles and genres is a testament to the power of artistic exploration. By weaving together influences from her musical upbringing, engaging in cross-genre collaborations, and strategically navigating the challenges of genre fluidity, Dabin not only enriched her own artistry but also contributed to the creation of Neon Frequencies' distinctive sound. This willingness to embrace diversity in music serves as an inspiration for aspiring musicians, reminding them that the beauty of music lies in its ability to transcend boundaries and connect people from all walks of life.

The Evolution of Dabin's Signature Sound

The journey of Dabin's musical evolution is a compelling narrative marked by exploration, innovation, and a relentless pursuit of artistic authenticity. As a musician deeply rooted in a rich tapestry of influences, Dabin's signature sound emerged as a unique blend of various genres, reflecting both personal experiences and broader musical trends.

Foundational Influences

Dabin's early exposure to diverse musical styles played a crucial role in shaping her sound. Growing up in a household where music was a constant presence, she absorbed influences from classical compositions to contemporary pop and electronic genres. This eclectic background laid the groundwork for her future explorations. The equation that encapsulates this formative influence can be expressed as:

$$S = \sum_{i=1}^{n} I_i$$

where S represents Dabin's signature sound, and I_i denotes the various influences she encountered throughout her life, with n being the total number of influences.

For instance, the intricate melodies of classical music provided Dabin with a foundation in harmony and structure, while the energetic beats of electronic dance music introduced her to rhythm and production techniques. This fusion of styles became the cornerstone of her musical identity.

FORMATIVE YEARS AND MUSICAL EDUCATION

Experimentation and Genre Blending

As Dabin progressed in her musical journey, she began to experiment with blending genres. Her willingness to push boundaries led to the creation of a sound that defied conventional categorization. This phase of experimentation can be represented by the equation:

$$E = f(G_1, G_2, G_3, \ldots, G_k)$$

where E is the evolution of her sound, and G_k represents the different genres she incorporated into her music. For example, Dabin seamlessly merged elements of pop, rock, and electronic music, resulting in tracks that resonate with a wide audience while maintaining her artistic integrity.

A notable example of this genre-blending is her hit single "Electric Heart," which combines the anthemic qualities of rock with the pulsating beats of electronic music. The song's structure features soaring guitar riffs layered over synthesized melodies, creating a dynamic soundscape that captures the listener's attention.

Technological Advancements and Sound Design

The evolution of Dabin's sound was also influenced by advancements in music technology. The emergence of digital audio workstations (DAWs) and innovative sound design techniques allowed her to explore new sonic possibilities. The relationship between technology and sound can be expressed through the following equation:

$$T = \frac{D}{R}$$

where T represents the technological influence on her sound, D is the diversity of sounds available through technology, and R is the rate of experimentation with these sounds.

Dabin's use of synthesizers, samplers, and effects processing exemplifies her embrace of technology. Her track "Galactic Voyage" showcases intricate sound layers created through extensive manipulation of audio samples, resulting in a rich auditory experience that transports listeners to otherworldly realms.

Lyrical Depth and Personal Narrative

Beyond the sonic elements, Dabin's signature sound is characterized by its lyrical depth and personal narrative. Her lyrics often reflect her experiences, emotions, and observations, adding a layer of authenticity to her music. The connection between her sound and lyrical content can be represented as:

$$L = g(S, N)$$

where L is the lyrical depth, S is the signature sound, and N represents the narrative elements embedded within her songs.

For example, in her song "Shattered Dreams," Dabin explores themes of heartbreak and resilience, with lyrics that resonate deeply with listeners. The raw emotion conveyed through her vocal delivery complements the musical arrangement, enhancing the overall impact of the track.

Collaboration and Collective Creativity

Collaboration has played a significant role in the evolution of Dabin's sound. Working with other artists and producers has opened new avenues for creativity and innovation. The collaborative process can be expressed as:

$$C = \sum_{j=1}^{m}(A_j + P_j)$$

where C represents the collective creativity resulting from collaboration, A_j denotes the artistic contributions of each collaborator, and P_j represents the production elements introduced by producers.

Dabin's collaboration with renowned producer Alex Turner on the album "Echoes of Tomorrow" resulted in a transformative sound that combined her signature style with Turner's innovative production techniques. The track "Reflections" exemplifies this synergy, showcasing a seamless integration of their artistic visions.

Conclusion: A Continual Journey

The evolution of Dabin's signature sound is an ongoing journey marked by exploration, experimentation, and collaboration. As she continues to push boundaries and embrace new influences, her music remains a testament to her artistic growth and resilience. The dynamic nature of her sound ensures that it will continue to evolve, captivating audiences and inspiring future generations of musicians.

In summary, Dabin's signature sound is a complex interplay of influences, technological advancements, lyrical depth, and collaborative creativity, all of which contribute to her unique musical identity. The evolution of her sound is not merely a reflection of her past but a promise of the innovative music to come.

A Match Made in Musical Heaven

Meeting the Bandmates: Destiny or Coincidence?

In the vibrant tapestry of the music world, the convergence of talent often feels like a cosmic event—a serendipitous meeting of souls destined to create magic together. For Dabin, the formation of Neon Frequencies was not just a mere coincidence but a perfect alignment of dreams, aspirations, and musical prowess. This section delves into the intricate dynamics of how Dabin met her bandmates, exploring whether their union was shaped by fate or simply the result of chance encounters.

The Prelude to Connection

Dabin's journey into the world of music was marked by a relentless pursuit of her passion. Growing up in a household where melodies danced through the air, she was destined to find her place in the music industry. However, the question loomed: who would share this journey with her? The universe had its plans, and it began with an open mic night at a local café, a seemingly mundane event that would change the course of her life forever.

The First Encounter

It was on a rainy Friday evening when Dabin took the stage, her heart racing with anticipation. The café was packed, the air thick with the smell of coffee and the sound of clinking glasses. As she strummed her guitar and poured her soul into the lyrics, she caught the attention of several aspiring musicians in the audience. Among them were Alex, a charismatic drummer with a penchant for rhythm, and Mia, a soulful bassist whose groove could make even the stiffest crowd sway.

Their admiration for Dabin's performance sparked an immediate connection. After her set, the trio found themselves huddled together, sharing stories of their musical journeys and dreams. It was as if they had known each other for lifetimes, their energies intertwining in a way that felt both familiar and exhilarating. This initial encounter laid the groundwork for what would become a powerful musical alliance.

Fate or Coincidence?

The question of whether their meeting was orchestrated by fate or mere coincidence is a philosophical one. From a psychological standpoint, the concept of *confirmation bias* suggests that individuals often interpret events in a way that confirms their beliefs or desires. Dabin, having longed for a musical partnership, might have viewed this encounter as destiny, whereas others might argue it was simply a fortunate accident.

To explore this further, we can consider the *Law of Attraction*, which posits that like attracts like; individuals who share similar energies and intentions are drawn to one another. In this light, Dabin, Alex, and Mia's shared passion for music and their collective aspirations could be seen as a magnetic force that brought them together.

$$F = G\frac{m_1 m_2}{r^2} \qquad (12)$$

In this equation, F represents the gravitational force between two masses m_1 and m_2 separated by a distance r. Analogously, the gravitational pull of their shared musical ambitions created a force that drew them together, regardless of whether it was destiny or coincidence.

The Spark of Collaboration

As the trio began to collaborate, the chemistry was undeniable. Their first jam session was a whirlwind of creativity, with each member contributing their unique style and energy. Dabin's ethereal vocals intertwined seamlessly with Alex's dynamic drumming and Mia's rhythmic bass lines, creating a sound that was fresh and invigorating.

This collaborative spirit was reminiscent of the famous saying, "The whole is greater than the sum of its parts." The synergy they experienced in those early days was a testament to the power of collaboration in music. Each member brought their strengths to the table, creating a unique sound that resonated with audiences.

The Role of Chance Encounters

While the trio's initial meeting felt fated, it is essential to acknowledge the role of chance encounters in the music industry. Many successful bands have emerged from random connections—friends of friends, chance meetings at parties, or even social media interactions. These serendipitous moments often lead to collaborations that change the trajectory of artists' careers.

For instance, consider the story of Fleetwood Mac, whose members came together through a series of chance encounters and relationships. Their unique blend of talents and personalities created a musical legacy that endures to this day.

Conclusion: A Harmonious Blend of Destiny and Coincidence

In the end, the meeting of Dabin and her bandmates was a beautiful blend of destiny and coincidence. Their shared passion for music and the cosmic alignment of their paths resulted in a powerful collaboration that would give birth to Neon Frequencies. Whether it was fate that brought them together or simply a fortunate twist of chance, one thing is clear: their union was destined to create waves in the music industry, leaving an indelible mark on the hearts of fans worldwide.

As Dabin reflects on those early days, she often marvels at the serendipity of their meeting, recognizing that sometimes, the universe conspires to bring together the right people at the right time. The journey of Neon Frequencies had only just begun, but the foundation laid during that fateful night would propel them toward greatness, proving that in the world of music, destiny and coincidence often dance hand in hand.

The Chemistry and Dynamic of the Band

The chemistry and dynamic of a band are crucial elements that contribute to its success and longevity in the music industry. Just like the perfect blend of ingredients in a recipe, the combination of personalities, talents, and creative energies among band members can lead to an explosive and harmonious musical experience. In this section, we will explore the various factors that define the chemistry and dynamics of Neon Frequencies, analyzing how these elements have played a significant role in shaping their unique sound and identity.

Understanding Band Chemistry

Band chemistry can be understood through the lens of social dynamics and interpersonal relationships. According to Tuckman's stages of group development, teams typically progress through four stages: forming, storming, norming, and performing. Each stage presents its own set of challenges and opportunities for growth.

Stage 1: Forming → Stage 2: Storming → Stage 3: Norming → Stage 4: Performing

(13)

During the forming stage, band members get to know one another, establishing initial relationships and roles. This stage is characterized by excitement and anticipation, but it can also lead to misunderstandings as individuals navigate their new environment. In the case of Neon Frequencies, the initial meetings between Dabin and the other band members were marked by a shared passion for music, leading to an immediate sense of connection.

The storming phase often brings conflict as members assert their opinions and creative visions. Neon Frequencies experienced this phase when trying to define their sound. Different influences and artistic directions led to heated discussions, but ultimately, these conflicts became a catalyst for innovation. For instance, during one jam session, a disagreement over the arrangement of a song resulted in a breakthrough moment where they fused their diverse influences into a new, distinctive sound.

The norming stage follows, where the band members begin to resolve their differences and establish a cohesive working relationship. This is where the chemistry truly begins to flourish. Dabin's ability to mediate and encourage collaboration among the band members helped solidify their dynamic, allowing each member to contribute their strengths while respecting one another's creative input.

Finally, the performing stage is where the band reaches its peak. The synergy among the members translates into electrifying live performances, captivating audiences and creating unforgettable experiences. Neon Frequencies achieved this stage through countless hours of rehearsals, where they honed their skills and developed an intuitive understanding of each other's musical instincts.

The Role of Individual Personalities

The individual personalities of band members significantly impact the overall chemistry. Each member brings unique traits, influences, and artistic sensibilities to the table, creating a rich tapestry of creativity. In Neon Frequencies, Dabin's leadership and vision serve as the backbone of the band, guiding their creative direction while fostering an environment of collaboration.

Research in psychology highlights the importance of personality compatibility in group dynamics. The Myers-Briggs Type Indicator (MBTI) categorizes individuals into 16 personality types, providing insights into how different personalities interact. For example, a band with a mix of extroverted and introverted members can create a balance between energetic performances and thoughtful songwriting.

In Neon Frequencies, the extroverted members thrive during live shows, engaging with the audience and creating an exhilarating atmosphere. Conversely, the more introspective members contribute to the songwriting process, delving into deeper themes and emotions. This balance allows the band to connect with fans on multiple levels, both through high-energy performances and poignant lyrics.

Creative Collaboration

Collaboration is at the heart of a band's chemistry. The process of co-writing songs and sharing creative ideas fosters a sense of unity and mutual respect. In Neon Frequencies, collaborative songwriting sessions often begin with a simple musical idea or a lyrical concept. For instance, during one session, Dabin brought in a guitar riff that sparked a flurry of creativity among the members.

$$\text{Songwriting Process} = \text{Initial Idea} + \text{Collaborative Input} \rightarrow \text{Final Composition} \tag{14}$$

As the band members contribute their thoughts and ideas, the initial concept evolves into a fully realized song. This process not only strengthens their bond but also enriches their sound, as each member's unique perspective is woven into the fabric of the music.

Moreover, the dynamic of the band is often influenced by external factors, such as the music industry and audience expectations. Navigating these pressures requires a strong foundation of trust and communication among band members. Neon Frequencies has demonstrated resilience in the face of challenges, often using external feedback to refine their sound while staying true to their artistic vision.

Examples of Chemistry in Action

Several memorable moments exemplify the chemistry and dynamic of Neon Frequencies. One standout instance occurred during a live performance at a local festival. The band was performing their hit single when an unexpected technical issue caused a brief pause. Instead of panicking, the members quickly improvised, engaging the audience with a spontaneous jam session that showcased their musical synergy. This moment not only highlighted their ability to adapt but also deepened the connection with their fans, leaving a lasting impression.

Another example is the creative process behind their debut album. During the recording sessions, the band faced numerous obstacles, including differing opinions on song arrangements. However, these challenges led to innovative solutions, as members pushed each other to explore new sounds and arrangements. The result was a debut album that not only captured their essence but also showcased their growth as a cohesive unit.

Conclusion

The chemistry and dynamic of Neon Frequencies are integral to their identity as a band. Through the stages of group development, the unique personalities of each member, and their collaborative efforts, they have created a musical legacy that resonates with fans worldwide. As they continue to evolve, the strength of their chemistry will undoubtedly remain a driving force behind their success.

In summary, the interplay of individual talents, personalities, and collaborative spirit defines the essence of Neon Frequencies, making them a formidable force in the music industry. Their journey exemplifies how a strong dynamic can lead to groundbreaking music and unforgettable experiences for both the band and their fans.

Jam Sessions: The Birth of their Unique Sound

The essence of *Neon Frequencies* was forged in the crucible of spontaneous creativity known as jam sessions. These informal gatherings became the heartbeat of the band, where ideas flowed as freely as the music itself. It was here, amidst the chords and rhythms, that the unique sound of *Neon Frequencies* began to take shape, blending various influences into a cohesive musical identity.

The Dynamics of Jam Sessions

Jam sessions serve as a melting pot of musical ideas, allowing band members to explore their creativity without the constraints of structured songwriting. The dynamics within these sessions are crucial; they foster collaboration and experimentation. As noted by music theorist John Zorn, "Improvisation is the ultimate expression of freedom in music." This philosophy resonated deeply with the members of *Neon Frequencies*, who embraced the opportunity to push boundaries.

The chemistry among band members was palpable during these sessions. Each musician brought their own influences, creating a rich tapestry of sound. For instance, Dabin's background in electronic music intertwined seamlessly with the rock and jazz elements introduced by the other members. This cross-pollination of genres led to the development of their signature sound, characterized by lush synths, intricate guitar riffs, and infectious grooves.

The Creative Process: A Case Study

To illustrate the creative process, let's examine a specific jam session that laid the groundwork for one of their hit tracks. During a particularly energetic session, Dabin began experimenting with a new synthesizer patch, producing a sound reminiscent of shimmering neon lights. The other band members quickly picked up on this vibe, layering their instruments over the synth line.

The equation for the harmonic structure can be represented as follows:

$$H(t) = \sum_{n=1}^{N} A_n \sin(2\pi f_n t + \phi_n) \qquad (15)$$

Where: - $H(t)$ is the harmonic output at time t, - A_n represents the amplitude of each frequency component, - f_n is the frequency of the nth harmonic, - ϕ_n is the phase shift of the nth harmonic.

As the session progressed, the band members began to interact with one another, responding to each other's musical cues. This led to the emergence of a distinctive groove, underscored by a syncopated bassline and dynamic percussion. The interplay between the instruments was not merely additive; rather, it created a complex web of sound that was both innovative and engaging.

Challenges and Breakthroughs

While jam sessions were a source of inspiration, they were not without challenges. The lack of structure sometimes led to moments of disarray, where ideas clashed rather than converged. However, these challenges often resulted in breakthroughs. By navigating through disagreements and experimenting with different arrangements, the band members learned to trust one another's instincts.

One memorable instance involved a disagreement over the tempo of a new piece. Tensions ran high as each member advocated for their preferred speed. Ultimately, they decided to meet in the middle, resulting in a tempo that was both energetic and danceable. This compromise not only enhanced the song but also solidified the band's collaborative spirit.

The Birth of a Unique Sound

The culmination of these jam sessions was the birth of *Neon Frequencies'* unique sound. By blending various genres and influences, they created a musical identity that resonated with fans across the globe. Their sound can be described as an eclectic mix of electronic, rock, and pop, characterized by catchy hooks, emotive lyrics, and a polished production style.

For example, the hit single "Electric Dreams" emerged directly from a jam session, where the band captured the exhilarating energy of their creative process. The fusion of Dabin's electronic elements with the band's organic instrumentation resulted in a track that was both innovative and accessible. The song's success on the charts was a testament to the power of collaboration and the magic that can happen when musicians come together in a spirit of creativity.

Conclusion

In conclusion, the jam sessions of *Neon Frequencies* were instrumental in shaping their musical identity. These gatherings not only fostered creativity but also strengthened the bonds between band members. The unique sound that emerged from these sessions continues to resonate with fans, proving that sometimes, the most extraordinary music is born from the simplest of beginnings. As the band reflects on their journey, they recognize that it was in these moments of improvisation and collaboration that their true artistry flourished, paving the way for a bright future in the music industry.

Creative Collaborations and Songwriting Magic

The journey of Neon Frequencies is marked by an alchemical blend of creativity, spontaneity, and synergy among its members. In the realm of music, collaboration often serves as the crucible where individual talents meld into something greater than the sum of their parts. For Dabin and her bandmates, this process was not just a method of songwriting; it was a magical experience that transformed their music and solidified their identity as a band.

The Essence of Collaboration

Collaboration in music is akin to a complex equation where each variable represents a unique musical influence, style, or idea. The equation can be simplified to:

$$C = \sum_{i=1}^{n}(M_i + I_i + E_i)$$

where C is the collaborative output, M_i represents the musical contributions of each member, I_i signifies individual influences, and E_i denotes the emotional input each member brings to the table. This collaborative equation encapsulates the essence of Neon Frequencies' songwriting process.

Finding Common Ground

From the moment Dabin met her bandmates, a shared vision began to take shape. The initial jam sessions, often spontaneous and unplanned, became the breeding ground for creativity. These sessions were characterized by a free exchange of ideas, where no thought was too outlandish and no riff too unconventional. The band members drew from a multitude of genres—rock, electronic, and classical—to create a sound that was uniquely theirs.

One notable example of this synergy occurred during the creation of their hit single, "Electric Dreams." Dabin, inspired by her childhood idols, brought a melodic hook that was both haunting and uplifting. Meanwhile, the drummer, Alex, infused the track with a driving rhythm that echoed the pulse of a heartbeat. The guitarist, Sam, layered intricate riffs that added depth and texture, while bassist Mia anchored the song with a groove that was impossible to ignore.

Songwriting Techniques

The songwriting techniques employed by Neon Frequencies were as diverse as their influences. Dabin often utilized a method known as "collaborative lyricism," where each band member contributed lines or themes based on personal experiences. This technique not only enriched the lyrics but also fostered a sense of ownership among the members.

For instance, in the song "Chasing Shadows," the lyrics reflect the struggles and triumphs of each member, weaving a narrative that resonates with listeners on multiple levels. The chorus, written collaboratively, encapsulates the essence of their shared journey:

> Chasing shadows, we rise and fall, Together we stand, united we call.

This lyrical approach ensured that every song carried the weight of their collective experiences, making the music relatable and authentic.

Overcoming Creative Blocks

Like any artistic endeavor, the process of collaboration was not without its challenges. Creative blocks often threatened to derail the momentum of songwriting sessions. However, the band learned to embrace these obstacles as opportunities for growth.

One effective strategy they employed was the "musical brainstorming" technique. During these sessions, the band would set a timer and write down as many musical ideas as possible within a limited timeframe. This approach not only sparked creativity but also alleviated the pressure of perfection, allowing ideas to flow freely.

For example, during the writing of their second album, the band faced a particularly challenging block. Instead of succumbing to frustration, they decided to host a "musical retreat" in a secluded cabin. This change of scenery, combined with a focused approach to brainstorming, resulted in the creation of several tracks that would ultimately define their sound.

The Role of Technology in Collaboration

In the modern music landscape, technology plays a pivotal role in facilitating collaboration. Neon Frequencies embraced digital tools that allowed them to share ideas and recordings in real-time, regardless of their physical location. Software such as Ableton Live and Logic Pro became essential in their creative process, enabling them to experiment with different sounds and arrangements.

The band also utilized cloud-based platforms for lyric writing and arrangement, allowing each member to contribute from anywhere in the world. This technological integration not only streamlined their workflow but also expanded their creative horizons.

Creating a Unique Sound

The culmination of their collaborative efforts resulted in a distinctive sound that set Neon Frequencies apart from their contemporaries. By blending various influences and styles, the band crafted a sonic landscape that was both innovative and familiar.

Their signature sound, characterized by ethereal synths, pulsating beats, and emotive lyrics, became a hallmark of their identity. Tracks like "Neon Nights" and "Euphoria" exemplified this unique sound, showcasing the band's ability to seamlessly merge genres while maintaining their artistic integrity.

The Impact of Collaboration on Legacy

Ultimately, the creative collaborations within Neon Frequencies not only shaped their music but also forged unbreakable bonds among the band members. This camaraderie became a driving force behind their success and a source of inspiration for their fans.

As Dabin reflected on their journey, she recognized that the magic of collaboration was not merely about creating music; it was about building a community. The stories, struggles, and triumphs shared within the band became the foundation of their legacy, leaving an indelible mark on the music industry and inspiring future generations of artists.

In conclusion, the creative collaborations and songwriting magic that defined Neon Frequencies served as a testament to the power of unity in artistic expression. Through their collective talents, the band not only crafted unforgettable music but also created a lasting impact that will resonate for years to come.

Solidifying the Band's Lineup

The journey of a band is often marked by the chemistry and dynamics among its members. In the case of Neon Frequencies, the process of solidifying the lineup was not merely a matter of finding talented musicians; it was about creating a cohesive unit that could create magic together. This section delves into the intricacies of how Neon Frequencies established its lineup, the challenges faced, and the successes achieved.

The Search for the Right Fit

Finding the perfect bandmates is akin to solving a complex equation where each variable must complement the others. The initial phase involved auditions, where potential members showcased their skills. However, it became clear that technical proficiency alone was insufficient. As Dabin noted, "It's not just about how well you play; it's about how well you connect with each other." This sentiment reflects the importance of interpersonal dynamics, which can be articulated through the following equation:

$$C = f(T, E, I) \tag{16}$$

where C represents the chemistry among band members, T is the technical skill level, E is emotional intelligence, and I is interpersonal compatibility. The ideal band lineup would maximize C while ensuring that the other variables are balanced.

The Dynamics of Collaboration

Once the initial lineup was formed, the next challenge was fostering a collaborative environment. The band engaged in numerous jam sessions, which served as both a testing ground for their sound and a way to build relationships. These sessions were not without conflict; differing musical tastes often led to creative disagreements. However, it was through navigating these challenges that the band found its unique voice.

A study on group dynamics in creative settings suggests that productive conflict can lead to innovation, as long as it is managed effectively. For Neon Frequencies, this meant establishing ground rules for collaboration, which included:

- Encouraging open dialogue about musical ideas.
- Setting aside time for experimentation without judgment.
- Regularly revisiting their shared vision and goals.

Defining Roles and Responsibilities

As the band began to solidify, it became crucial to define each member's role clearly. This not only helped streamline the creative process but also minimized potential conflicts. Each member brought unique strengths to the table—Dabin's prowess in songwriting, the guitarist's flair for improvisation, and the drummer's impeccable timing.

The roles could be summarized in the following matrix:

$$\text{Roles} = \begin{bmatrix} \text{Songwriting} & \text{Instrumentation} & \text{Vocals} \\ \text{Dabin} & \text{Guitarist} & \text{Vocalist} \\ \text{Lyricist} & \text{Drummer} & \text{Producer} \end{bmatrix} \qquad (17)$$

This matrix not only clarified responsibilities but also highlighted the interdependencies among members, reinforcing the idea that each role was vital for the band's success.

Building a Shared Vision

A crucial aspect of solidifying the lineup was the establishment of a shared vision. The band collectively envisioned a sound that blended various genres, drawing inspiration from their diverse musical backgrounds. This vision was encapsulated in their mission statement: "To create music that resonates with the soul, transcending genres and connecting with audiences worldwide."

The alignment of personal and collective goals can be represented by the following equation:

$$V = \sum_{i=1}^{n} G_i \qquad (18)$$

where V is the shared vision, G_i represents the individual goals of each band member, and n is the number of members. The success of Neon Frequencies hinged on their ability to harmonize these individual aspirations into a singular, powerful vision.

The Role of Trust and Respect

Trust and respect emerged as foundational elements in solidifying the band's lineup. In the high-pressure environment of the music industry, these qualities fostered a sense of safety that encouraged creativity. The band members engaged in team-building exercises, both on and off the stage, to strengthen their relationships.

Research in organizational behavior indicates that trust enhances collaboration and leads to higher performance outcomes. For Neon Frequencies, this meant that as trust grew, so did their ability to take creative risks, leading to innovative songwriting and performances.

Finalizing the Lineup

Ultimately, the solidification of Neon Frequencies' lineup was the result of a combination of chemistry, collaboration, clearly defined roles, a shared vision, and mutual trust. The culmination of these elements led to the creation of a band that was not only talented but also resilient and adaptable.

As they prepared for their first major performance, the members of Neon Frequencies reflected on their journey. Dabin remarked, "We've built something special here. It's not just about the music; it's about the bond we share." This realization underscored the importance of the foundational work they had done to solidify their lineup, setting the stage for the incredible journey that lay ahead.

In conclusion, the solidification of Neon Frequencies' lineup was a multifaceted process that involved careful consideration of interpersonal dynamics, collaborative practices, and the establishment of a shared vision. Through dedication and a commitment to each other, they transformed from a group of musicians into a cohesive band ready to take on the world.

The Creative Process: From Studio to Stage

Writing, Recording, and Refining Songs

The journey of creating music is a multifaceted process that blends creativity, technical skill, and emotional expression. For Dabin and Neon Frequencies, writing, recording, and refining songs is not merely a task; it is an art form that evolves with each project. This section delves into the intricate layers of songwriting, the challenges faced during recording sessions, and the meticulous refinement that transforms initial ideas into polished tracks.

The Songwriting Process

Songwriting is the backbone of any musical endeavor. It begins with an idea, a spark of inspiration that can stem from personal experiences, societal observations, or even abstract concepts. The process can be broken down into several key components:

- **Lyric Writing:** Dabin often draws from personal narratives, utilizing vivid imagery and emotional depth to connect with listeners. The lyrics serve as the narrative thread of the song, guiding the listener through the intended experience. For instance, in the song "Echoes of Tomorrow", the lyrics explore themes of nostalgia and hope, creating a poignant juxtaposition that resonates with fans.

- **Melody Composition:** The melody is the soul of a song. Dabin's approach to melody involves experimenting with different scales and modes to evoke specific emotions. The use of the pentatonic scale, for example, can create a sense of longing, while the major scale often conveys joy and triumph.

- **Harmonic Structure:** The harmonic foundation of a song is crucial for establishing its mood. Dabin often employs chord progressions that are both familiar and innovative. A classic example is the I-IV-V-vi progression, which provides a sense of resolution while allowing for creative variations that keep the listener engaged.

- **Arrangement:** Once the core elements are established, the arrangement comes into play. This involves deciding on the instrumentation, dynamics, and overall structure of the song. Dabin and the band often discuss the arrangement collaboratively, ensuring that each member's input is valued and integrated into the final product.

Recording Techniques

Recording is where the magic truly begins to take shape. The studio environment serves as a canvas for the band to paint their sonic masterpiece. Here are some key aspects of their recording process:

- **Pre-Production:** Before stepping into the studio, Dabin and the band engage in thorough pre-production sessions. This phase includes rehearsals, refining song structures, and making critical decisions about instrumentation. They often create demo recordings to capture the essence of each song, allowing for further exploration of ideas.

- **Tracking:** During tracking, each instrument is recorded separately, allowing for a clean and polished sound. Dabin emphasizes the importance of capturing the energy of each performance. For example, while recording the guitar tracks for *"Chasing Shadows"*, they utilized a combination of direct input and microphone techniques to achieve a rich, layered sound.

- **Vocal Recording:** The vocals are often recorded last, allowing Dabin to infuse the final performance with the emotional weight of the completed instrumental tracks. Techniques such as double tracking and harmonization are employed to create a fuller vocal sound.

- **Editing:** Post-tracking, the editing phase begins. This involves cleaning up the recorded tracks, adjusting timing issues, and ensuring that each element fits seamlessly within the mix. Dabin often collaborates with sound engineers to refine the sound, utilizing digital audio workstations (DAWs) to manipulate audio with precision.

Refinement and Mixing

Once the initial recording is complete, the refinement process begins. This stage is crucial for achieving a polished final product:

- **Mixing:** Mixing involves balancing the levels of each instrument and vocal track, applying effects such as reverb and compression to enhance the overall sound. Dabin believes that mixing is akin to painting; each element must be carefully placed to create a harmonious whole.

- **Mastering:** The final step in the production process is mastering, which prepares the track for distribution. This involves ensuring that the song sounds cohesive across all playback systems. Dabin often works with experienced mastering engineers to achieve the best possible sound quality.

- **Feedback and Iteration:** Throughout the entire process, feedback is invaluable. Dabin and the band regularly seek input from trusted peers and mentors, using constructive criticism to refine their work further. This iterative process can lead to significant changes, often resulting in a song that far exceeds its original conception.

Challenges in the Process

Despite the excitement of creating music, the process is not without its challenges:

- **Creative Blocks:** Every artist faces creative blocks at some point. Dabin has found that stepping away from a project or seeking inspiration from other art forms can help overcome these hurdles.

- **Technical Difficulties:** Recording sessions can be fraught with technical issues, from equipment malfunctions to software glitches. Dabin emphasizes the importance of being adaptable and resourceful in the face of such challenges.

- **Collaboration Dynamics:** While collaboration can lead to amazing outcomes, it can also present difficulties. Differing artistic visions and personalities can create tension within the band. Dabin encourages open communication and compromise to navigate these dynamics effectively.

In conclusion, the process of writing, recording, and refining songs is a complex yet rewarding journey for Dabin and Neon Frequencies. Through collaboration, experimentation, and perseverance, they transform raw ideas into captivating musical experiences that resonate with fans worldwide. Each song is a testament to their dedication and passion for the art of music, reflecting their growth as artists and their commitment to pushing the boundaries of sound.

Pushing Boundaries: Experimentation and Innovation

In the world of music, pushing boundaries is not just an act of creativity; it is a necessity for evolution. For Dabin and Neon Frequencies, this principle became a cornerstone of their artistic journey. The band embraced experimentation and innovation, allowing them to carve out a distinctive sound that resonated with fans and critics alike. This section delves into the theoretical underpinnings of musical experimentation, the challenges faced, and the innovative techniques employed by the band.

Theoretical Framework of Musical Experimentation

Musical experimentation can be understood through the lens of various theories, including the *Theory of Creativity* and the *Aesthetic Experience Theory*. The Theory of Creativity posits that innovation arises from the interplay of knowledge, skills, and imaginative thinking. This is particularly relevant in music, where artists draw from a vast pool of influences and techniques to create something novel.

The Aesthetic Experience Theory, on the other hand, emphasizes the emotional response elicited by art. Dabin and the band recognized that innovation is not merely about technical prowess; it is about crafting experiences that evoke feelings and provoke thought. The integration of these theories informed their approach to experimentation.

Challenges of Innovation

While the desire to innovate is often fueled by passion, it comes with its own set of challenges. One significant problem is the risk of alienating existing fans. As artists venture into uncharted territory, there is a potential for backlash from audiences who prefer their earlier work. Dabin faced this dilemma when introducing new elements to the band's sound, such as electronic influences and unconventional song structures.

Moreover, the technical aspects of experimentation can pose significant hurdles. Incorporating new instruments or production techniques requires not only a willingness to learn but also the ability to adapt to new workflows. The band had to navigate these complexities while maintaining their core identity.

Innovative Techniques Employed by Dabin

Dabin's approach to experimentation involved several innovative techniques that pushed the boundaries of traditional music-making. One notable example is the incorporation of *live-looping* during performances. This technique involves recording audio in real-time and layering it to create a rich, textured sound. By utilizing live-looping, Dabin was able to create intricate soundscapes that captivated audiences and showcased her musical versatility.

In addition to live-looping, Dabin and her bandmates explored the use of *found sounds*—everyday noises that are recorded and manipulated to create unique sonic elements. This technique not only added depth to their music but also aligned with the growing trend of *sound art*, blurring the lines between music and visual art.

Another innovative approach was the use of *cross-genre collaborations*. Dabin sought out artists from diverse musical backgrounds, resulting in a fusion of styles that expanded the band's sonic palette. Collaborating with electronic producers, classical musicians, and even visual artists, Neon Frequencies created a multi-dimensional experience that transcended conventional genre boundaries.

Case Study: The Album "Elysium"

The culmination of Dabin's experimental efforts is best illustrated in the album *Elysium*. This project served as a testament to the band's commitment to innovation. The album features a blend of electronic, rock, and orchestral elements, showcasing the versatility of Dabin's songwriting and production skills.

A standout track, "Echoes of Tomorrow," exemplifies the band's innovative spirit. The song begins with a haunting piano melody, gradually layered with synthesized sounds and intricate percussion. The incorporation of a string quartet adds an unexpected depth, demonstrating the band's ability to merge disparate musical elements seamlessly.

The recording process for *Elysium* was marked by a willingness to experiment with unconventional recording techniques. For instance, the band recorded certain tracks in unique environments, such as an abandoned warehouse, to capture the raw acoustics and ambiance. This approach not only enhanced the sound quality but also infused the music with a sense of place and authenticity.

Conclusion

In conclusion, Dabin and Neon Frequencies exemplified the power of pushing boundaries through experimentation and innovation. By embracing theoretical frameworks, overcoming challenges, and employing inventive techniques, they were able to create a sound that resonated with a diverse audience. Their journey serves as a reminder that true artistic growth often lies beyond the comfort zone, and that the willingness to explore the unknown can lead to remarkable musical achievements.

Studio Sessions: Challenges and Victories

Recording in the studio is often romanticized as a magical experience where creativity flows freely and the perfect sound is just a few tweaks away. However, for Dabin and the Neon Frequencies, the reality of studio sessions was a rollercoaster ride filled with challenges, victories, and moments of sheer brilliance. Each session was a testament to their resilience and passion for music.

The Pressure of Perfection

One of the most significant challenges faced during studio sessions was the pressure to produce a flawless recording. The band often found themselves grappling with the fear of not meeting the expectations set by their burgeoning fan base and the music industry. This pressure can be likened to the phenomenon known as *performance anxiety*, which can lead to overthinking and self-doubt.

In one notable session, the band was working on a track that was meant to be the lead single for their debut album. After countless takes, the energy in the room began to wane. The producer, sensing the frustration, decided to take a break. During this break, they engaged in a spontaneous jam session, which rekindled their creativity and led to the birth of a new song that would become a fan favorite. This incident highlighted the importance of taking a step back and allowing creativity to flow organically.

Technical Difficulties

Technical issues were another common hurdle during recording sessions. From equipment malfunctions to software glitches, these challenges could derail the creative process. For instance, during the recording of their second album, the band experienced a catastrophic failure of their primary recording software just days before a major deadline.

To overcome this setback, the band had to adapt quickly. They utilized a backup system and even recorded some tracks using a mobile setup, demonstrating their ability to pivot under pressure. This adaptability not only saved the project but also resulted in a raw, authentic sound that resonated with their audience.

Collaboration and Compromise

Another vital aspect of the studio experience was the collaborative nature of their work. With each member bringing unique influences and ideas to the table, creative differences were inevitable. For example, during the recording of a particularly ambitious track, Dabin and one of the bandmates had conflicting visions regarding the song's arrangement.

To resolve this, they engaged in a constructive debate, weighing the pros and cons of each approach. This process is rooted in *collaborative creativity theory*, which posits that diverse perspectives can lead to innovative solutions. Ultimately, they found a middle ground that incorporated elements from both visions, resulting in a richer sound that showcased the band's dynamic range.

Recording Techniques and Innovations

The studio sessions also served as a playground for experimentation with recording techniques. Dabin and the band were not afraid to push boundaries and explore new sounds. They often employed unconventional methods, such as using everyday objects as instruments or layering sounds in unexpected ways.

One memorable instance involved using a wine glass filled with water to create ethereal sounds that were later incorporated into a track. This approach aligns with the concept of *sonic experimentation*, which encourages artists to explore sounds beyond traditional instruments. The result was a track that not only stood out sonically but also demonstrated the band's willingness to innovate.

Capturing the Essence of Neon Frequencies

Ultimately, the studio sessions were about capturing the essence of Neon Frequencies. Each challenge faced and victory achieved contributed to the band's unique sound. The lessons learned in the studio—resilience in the face of adversity, the power of collaboration, and the importance of innovation—shaped their identity as artists.

As they moved from the studio to the stage, the energy and passion cultivated during these sessions translated into electrifying live performances. The studio became a crucible of creativity, forging the sound that would define their career and resonate with fans around the world.

In conclusion, the studio sessions of Dabin and Neon Frequencies were a microcosm of their journey—filled with challenges that tested their resolve and victories that celebrated their creativity. Each recording not only marked a step in their musical evolution but also solidified their bond as a band, paving the way for the legacy they would leave in the music industry.

From Studio to Stage: Bringing the Music to Life

The transition from studio recording to live performance is a transformative journey that encapsulates the very essence of music. For Dabin and Neon Frequencies, this metamorphosis is not merely a logistical challenge but a creative odyssey that breathes life into their sound. In this section, we delve deep into the intricacies of this process, exploring the theories, challenges, and triumphs that define the band's live performances.

THE CREATIVE PROCESS: FROM STUDIO TO STAGE

Theoretical Foundations of Live Performance

At the heart of any live performance lies the concept of **musical interpretation**. This theory posits that a piece of music can take on various meanings and emotional weights depending on the context in which it is presented. In the studio, Dabin and her bandmates meticulously craft their sound, layering instruments and harmonies to create a polished recording. However, when it comes to live performances, the interpretation shifts dramatically.

One critical aspect of this shift is the **dynamic interaction** between the performers and the audience. According to *Sociomusical Theory*, the relationship between musicians and their audience can significantly influence the performance's energy and emotional impact. For instance, when Neon Frequencies plays a high-energy track, the band feeds off the audience's enthusiasm, which in turn amplifies the performance's intensity.

Challenges in Transitioning from Studio to Stage

Despite the excitement of performing live, several challenges arise during this transition. One significant issue is **sound fidelity**. In the studio, the band can manipulate sounds with precision, utilizing various effects and production techniques to achieve their desired outcome. However, replicating this sound in a live setting often proves difficult due to limitations in equipment and acoustics.

To illustrate this, consider the equation for sound pressure level (SPL):

$$SPL = 20\log_{10}\left(\frac{P}{P_0}\right) \qquad (19)$$

where P is the sound pressure of the sound wave and P_0 is the reference sound pressure (typically $20\,\mu Pa$). In a live setting, achieving the desired SPL while maintaining clarity and balance among instruments can be a formidable task.

Another challenge is the **performance anxiety** that can affect musicians. The pressure to deliver a flawless performance can lead to stress, which may hinder creativity and spontaneity. Dabin has often shared her experiences of facing stage fright, particularly during the early days of touring. To combat this, she employs various techniques, such as mindfulness and visualization, to center herself before stepping onto the stage.

Embracing the Live Experience

Despite these challenges, the thrill of live performance is unparalleled. The band approaches each show as an opportunity to connect with their audience on a deeper level. They often incorporate **improvisation** into their setlists, allowing for spontaneous moments that make each performance unique. This practice not only keeps the energy high but also showcases the musicians' versatility and creativity.

For example, during a performance of their hit single, Neon Frequencies might extend a particular section, allowing Dabin to showcase her skills on the guitar, while the band engages in a call-and-response with the audience. This interaction fosters a sense of community, transforming a concert into a shared experience.

The Role of Technology in Live Performances

In recent years, technology has played an increasingly crucial role in bridging the gap between studio recordings and live performances. The use of **digital audio workstations** (DAWs) and live looping equipment allows musicians to recreate complex arrangements on stage. Dabin, known for her innovative approach, often utilizes looping pedals to layer sounds live, creating a rich tapestry of music that mirrors the intricacies of their studio work.

Moreover, advancements in **sound engineering** have led to improved equipment that enhances live sound quality. The use of in-ear monitors, for instance, allows musicians to hear themselves and each other clearly, minimizing the risk of dissonance during performances. This technology has enabled Neon Frequencies to deliver a sound that is both faithful to their recordings and engaging for their audience.

Capturing the Essence of Neon Frequencies

Ultimately, the goal of transitioning from studio to stage is to capture the essence of Neon Frequencies and bring it to life for their fans. Each performance serves as a testament to their artistic journey, reflecting the hard work and dedication that has gone into their music. Through the challenges and triumphs of live performances, Dabin and her bandmates continue to evolve, pushing the boundaries of their sound while forging a profound connection with their audience.

In conclusion, the process of bringing music to life from the studio to the stage is a complex interplay of theory, practice, and emotion. Dabin's commitment to her craft, combined with the band's chemistry and the power of technology, ensures that each performance is a unique celebration of their artistic vision. As they continue to tour and inspire fans worldwide, the journey from studio to stage remains a cornerstone of Neon Frequencies' legacy.

THE CREATIVE PROCESS: FROM STUDIO TO STAGE

Capturing the Essence of Neon Frequencies: Recording their Iconic Debut Album

The journey to record the debut album of Neon Frequencies was nothing short of a thrilling rollercoaster ride, a blend of creativity, technical challenges, and sheer determination. The band, driven by the desire to encapsulate their unique sound, embarked on a mission that would ultimately define their identity in the music industry.

The Vision: Crafting the Sound

At the heart of this endeavor was Dabin's vision. She envisioned an album that would not only showcase the band's musical prowess but also resonate with listeners on a deeper emotional level. The goal was to create a sound that blended various genres—elements of electronic, rock, and pop—while maintaining a cohesive sonic identity. This led to the foundational question:

$$S = \sum_{i=1}^{n} w_i \cdot x_i \qquad (20)$$

where S represents the final sound, w_i are the weights assigned to different genres, and x_i are the individual sounds or elements being incorporated. This equation encapsulated their approach to sound design: a careful balance of influences that would culminate in a harmonious end product.

The Recording Process: Challenges and Triumphs

As the band entered the studio, they faced a myriad of challenges. The first hurdle was the technical aspect of recording. With various instruments and sounds to capture, the band had to navigate the complexities of studio acoustics and equipment. The initial sessions were fraught with issues—microphone placements that didn't capture the intended sound, and instrumental clashes that muddied their unique style.

To tackle these challenges, they employed the principle of *sound isolation*, which can be mathematically represented as:

$$I = \frac{P_{in}}{P_{out}} \qquad (21)$$

where I is the isolation factor, P_{in} is the incoming sound pressure level, and P_{out} is the outgoing sound pressure level. This principle guided their efforts to ensure that each instrument could be recorded distinctly, allowing for greater clarity in the final mix.

Creative Collaborations: The Magic of Teamwork

One of the most rewarding aspects of the recording process was the collaborative spirit within the band. Each member brought their own experiences and influences to the table, creating a melting pot of ideas. Dabin, known for her innovative songwriting, would often lead jam sessions that sparked creativity. These sessions were not just about playing music; they were about exploring new concepts and pushing the boundaries of their sound.

For example, during one session, the band experimented with a new electronic beat that combined traditional rock elements with modern synths. This fusion not only showcased their versatility but also led to the creation of their breakout single, which would later become a defining track on the album. The equation for their collaborative creativity could be viewed as:

$$C = \sum_{j=1}^{m} (e_j \cdot i_j) \tag{22}$$

where C is the creative output, e_j represents the individual efforts of each band member, and i_j denotes the ideas they contribute. This synergy was essential in capturing the essence of Neon Frequencies.

From Studio to Stage: Bringing the Music to Life

As the recording sessions progressed, the band began to focus on how to translate their studio sound to live performances. This required an understanding of the *performance dynamics*, which can be modeled as:

$$D = f(E, A, C) \tag{23}$$

where D is the dynamic performance level, E is the energy of the band, A is the audience engagement, and C is the complexity of the music. The band understood that their live shows needed to capture the same energy and emotion that their recordings did, leading to a series of rehearsals that emphasized not just technical proficiency but also emotional connection with the audience.

Capturing the Essence: The Final Mix

The final stage of recording involved mixing and mastering the album. This process was crucial in ensuring that every element of their sound was polished and balanced. The band worked closely with an experienced sound engineer, who helped them navigate the intricacies of audio mixing.

The mixing process can be expressed through the equation:

$$M = \frac{1}{N} \sum_{k=1}^{N} (L_k + E_k + A_k) \tag{24}$$

where M is the final mix, L_k is the level of each track, E_k is the equalization adjustments, and A_k represents the effects applied to each sound. This meticulous attention to detail ensured that their debut album would not only be a testament to their hard work but also a reflection of their artistic vision.

The Impact of the Debut Album

Upon its release, the debut album of Neon Frequencies resonated with fans and critics alike. It was celebrated for its innovative sound and emotional depth, capturing the essence of the band's journey. The album not only marked the beginning of their career but also set the stage for their future endeavors.

In conclusion, the recording of Neon Frequencies' iconic debut album was a multifaceted process that involved creativity, technical skill, and collaboration. Through challenges and triumphs, the band emerged with a sound that was distinctly their own, forever capturing the essence of their musical journey in a way that would inspire listeners worldwide.

The Rise of a Phenomenon

Early Performances and Local Hype

The journey of Neon Frequencies began in the vibrant local music scene, where the echoes of their early performances reverberated through intimate venues and community gatherings. This was not merely the launching pad of a band; it was the crucible where their sound was forged and their identity solidified. The local hype surrounding Neon Frequencies was not just a product of their talent, but also a testament to the magnetic energy they brought to every stage they graced.

In the initial phase, the band performed at various open mic nights and small bars, places where the walls were adorned with the memories of countless aspiring artists. Each performance was a unique experiment, a blend of their eclectic influences and the raw energy of their youthful exuberance. The chemistry among the bandmates was palpable, creating an atmosphere that was both electric and inviting. Their early setlists, though simple, were infused with a passion that drew audiences in, establishing a connection that transcended mere entertainment.

To understand the dynamics of their early performances, we can apply the concept of **audience engagement**, which can be represented by the equation:

$$E = \frac{A}{C}$$

where E is the engagement level, A is the audience's attention, and C is the competition for attention (which includes other distractions in the environment). In the case of Neon Frequencies, their ability to capture and maintain audience attention was exceptional, as they created an immersive experience that overshadowed the typical distractions of a bar setting.

As they played more shows, word began to spread. Local music blogs and social media platforms buzzed with excitement, creating a ripple effect that propelled Neon Frequencies into the spotlight. The band's unique sound, a fusion of electronic beats and organic melodies, was unlike anything the local scene had experienced. This innovative approach to music not only resonated with audiences but also attracted the attention of local influencers and event organizers.

One of the pivotal moments in their early career came during a local music festival, where they were given the opportunity to perform alongside established acts. This exposure was critical for building their reputation. The festival served as a microcosm of the larger music industry, showcasing the importance of networking and visibility. The equation of **visibility** can be illustrated as:

$$V = R \times P$$

where V represents visibility, R is the reach of promotional efforts, and P is the performance quality. Neon Frequencies excelled in both aspects, with their captivating performances combined with strategic social media marketing, leading to a significant increase in their visibility.

The response from the audience was overwhelming. Fans began to share their experiences on social media, using hashtags that would soon become synonymous with the band. The organic growth of their fanbase was a phenomenon worth analyzing; it reflected the power of community in the music industry. Local hype transformed into a dedicated following, with fans attending multiple shows and bringing friends along, creating a snowball effect that was crucial for their ascent.

THE RISE OF A PHENOMENON

Furthermore, the band's early performances were characterized by a deep understanding of **live music dynamics**. The interplay between the band and the audience can be described by the feedback loop:

$$F = I \times R$$

where F is the feedback received, I is the intensity of the performance, and R is the audience's reaction. Neon Frequencies mastered this loop, adjusting their setlists and stage presence based on real-time feedback from their audience. This adaptability not only enhanced their performances but also fostered a sense of community among their fans, who felt valued and heard.

In conclusion, the early performances of Neon Frequencies were more than just gigs; they were the foundation of a burgeoning musical phenomenon. The local hype that surrounded them was a product of their unique sound, engaging performances, and the organic growth of their fanbase. As they transitioned from local heroes to rising stars, these early experiences would shape their artistic direction and influence their future endeavors in the music industry. The blend of talent, hard work, and community support created a perfect storm that set the stage for their eventual success.

Building a Fan Base: The Power of Word of Mouth

In the music industry, the journey from obscurity to stardom often hinges on a single, powerful force: word of mouth. For Neon Frequencies, this organic form of promotion became the cornerstone of their burgeoning fan base. Word of mouth, defined as the informal exchange of information between individuals, operates on the principle that people trust recommendations from friends and family more than traditional advertising. This section delves into the mechanics of word of mouth, its significance in building a fan base, and the unique strategies employed by Neon Frequencies to harness this potent tool.

The Mechanics of Word of Mouth

The phenomenon of word of mouth can be quantified through the **Diffusion of Innovations** theory, which illustrates how new ideas and products gain momentum within a social system. According to Rogers (2003), the process involves five stages: knowledge, persuasion, decision, implementation, and confirmation. In the context of music, fans first gain *knowledge* of a band through friends or social media. This initial exposure can lead to *persuasion*, where the listener forms a positive opinion based on the enthusiasm of their peers.

The effectiveness of word of mouth can be mathematically represented using the **Bass Diffusion Model**:

$$N(t) = \frac{(p+q)^2}{p} \cdot \left(1 - e^{-(p+q)t}\right) \tag{25}$$

where: - $N(t)$ is the cumulative number of adopters at time t, - p is the coefficient of innovation (the likelihood that an individual will adopt the innovation based on external influences), - q is the coefficient of imitation (the likelihood that an individual will adopt the innovation based on the behavior of others).

For Neon Frequencies, the coefficients p and q were significantly influenced by their energetic live performances and the personal connections they fostered with fans.

Creating Buzz: Strategies Employed by Neon Frequencies

Neon Frequencies understood that to capitalize on word of mouth, they needed to create memorable experiences that fans would want to share. Here are some strategies they employed:

- **Engaging Live Performances:** The band made it a priority to deliver electrifying performances that left audiences buzzing. Each concert was designed to be a unique experience, complete with stunning visuals and unexpected surprises. This not only encouraged fans to talk about the shows but also to bring their friends to future gigs.

- **Social Media Interaction:** Neon Frequencies leveraged platforms like Instagram, Twitter, and TikTok to engage with fans directly. By sharing behind-the-scenes content, responding to fan messages, and encouraging user-generated content, they fostered a sense of community. This interaction acted as a catalyst for word of mouth, as fans felt personally connected to the band and eager to share their experiences online.

- **Exclusive Content and Promotions:** The band offered exclusive content, such as early access to new music or limited-edition merchandise, to fans who shared their music with others. This incentivized fans to spread the word, creating a ripple effect that expanded their reach.

- **Fan Involvement:** Neon Frequencies actively involved their fans in the creative process, inviting them to vote on setlists or participate in contests.

This sense of ownership made fans more likely to promote the band within their social circles.

Challenges in Word of Mouth Promotion

While word of mouth can be a powerful tool, it is not without its challenges. Miscommunication, negative experiences, or a lack of engagement can hinder a band's ability to build a loyal fan base. For Neon Frequencies, maintaining a consistent and positive image was crucial. They faced the challenge of ensuring that every interaction—whether online or in person—reflected their brand ethos.

Moreover, the digital age has transformed word of mouth into a double-edged sword. A single negative review can spread rapidly, potentially overshadowing the positive buzz generated by loyal fans. Therefore, Neon Frequencies had to be vigilant in monitoring their online presence and addressing any issues promptly.

Real-World Examples of Successful Word of Mouth Campaigns

Several artists have successfully harnessed the power of word of mouth to build their fan bases. For instance, the indie band *Mumford & Sons* rose to prominence largely through grassroots efforts and word of mouth. Their unique sound and engaging live performances led to fans sharing their music with friends, resulting in a snowball effect that propelled them into the mainstream.

Similarly, the rise of *Billie Eilish* can be attributed to the organic buzz generated by her early singles. Eilish's distinct style and relatable persona resonated with listeners, who eagerly recommended her music to others, leading to a rapid increase in her fan base.

Conclusion

In conclusion, the power of word of mouth played a pivotal role in building the fan base of Neon Frequencies. By creating memorable experiences, engaging with fans, and navigating the challenges of digital communication, the band was able to leverage this organic form of promotion effectively. As they continued to grow, the ripple effect of their passionate fans would serve as a testament to the enduring impact of word of mouth in the music industry.

Breaking into the Mainstream: Radio and Press Exposure

In the dynamic landscape of the music industry, breaking into the mainstream is akin to navigating a labyrinth of sound, media, and audience reception. For Neon

Frequencies, this journey was not merely a matter of luck; it was a calculated endeavor involving strategic radio play and press exposure that would catapult them into the limelight.

The Role of Radio in Music Promotion

Radio has long been a cornerstone of music promotion, serving as a bridge between artists and potential fans. The impact of radio airplay can be quantified by the following equation:

$$P = f(A, F, T) \qquad (26)$$

where P represents popularity, A stands for airplay frequency, F denotes the reach of the radio station, and T signifies the time of day the song is played. This equation highlights the multifaceted nature of radio promotion, where an increase in any of these variables can exponentially enhance an artist's visibility.

For Neon Frequencies, their breakthrough single was strategically placed in prime time slots on popular radio stations. The band's management understood that consistent airplay during peak hours would not only boost their popularity but also foster a sense of familiarity among listeners. This approach proved effective, as the single began to climb the charts, garnering attention from both fans and industry insiders.

Press Exposure: The Power of Media Coverage

While radio played a pivotal role in reaching listeners, press exposure was equally crucial in shaping public perception. The media landscape, comprising music blogs, magazines, and online platforms, serves as a powerful tool for storytelling and artist branding. For Neon Frequencies, the following factors were instrumental in securing press coverage:

- **Press Releases and EPKs:** The band crafted compelling press releases and electronic press kits (EPKs) that highlighted their unique sound, background, and the story behind their music. These materials were distributed to key journalists and influencers in the music scene.

- **Interviews and Features:** Securing interviews with influential music publications allowed the band to share their journey, influences, and aspirations. This personal touch resonated with readers and created a deeper connection with their audience.

- **Social Media Engagement:** In the digital age, social media platforms have become essential for promoting music and engaging with fans. Neon Frequencies utilized platforms like Instagram, Twitter, and Facebook to share behind-the-scenes content, updates, and interact with their growing fanbase.

The synergy between radio airplay and press exposure created a feedback loop that amplified Neon Frequencies' presence in the music industry. As their popularity soared, more media outlets began to take notice, resulting in features and interviews that further solidified their status as rising stars.

Challenges and Solutions in Gaining Exposure

Despite the strategic efforts, breaking into the mainstream was not without its challenges. The music industry is notoriously competitive, and many talented artists struggle to gain the attention they deserve. Neon Frequencies faced several hurdles, including:

- **Oversaturation of the Market:** With countless new artists emerging daily, standing out became increasingly difficult. To combat this, the band focused on refining their unique sound and branding, ensuring that their music resonated with listeners on a personal level.

- **Negative Press and Criticism:** Early reviews were mixed, with some critics questioning their authenticity. Instead of shying away from criticism, the band embraced it, using feedback to evolve their sound and prove their naysayers wrong.

- **Limited Resources:** As an emerging band, financial constraints posed a significant challenge in securing high-profile radio spots and press coverage. Neon Frequencies overcame this by leveraging grassroots marketing strategies, such as local performances and word-of-mouth promotion, to build a loyal fanbase.

Case Study: The Hit Single that Changed Everything

The turning point for Neon Frequencies came with the release of their hit single, "*Electric Dreams.*" This track exemplified their ability to blend genres, appealing to a broad audience. The combination of catchy hooks, relatable lyrics, and a vibrant sound captured the attention of both radio stations and music critics alike.

The song's rise to prominence can be illustrated through the following metrics:

- **Radio Play:** Within the first month of its release, *"Electric Dreams"* received over 1,000 spins on various radio stations across the country.

- **Press Coverage:** The single was featured in over 50 music blogs and magazines, including a prominent interview in *Rolling Stone*, which significantly boosted their visibility.

- **Social Media Engagement:** The hashtag #ElectricDreams trended on Twitter, generating thousands of tweets and shares, further amplifying their reach.

As a result of these combined efforts, Neon Frequencies not only broke into the mainstream but also established themselves as a formidable force in the music industry, paving the way for future successes.

In conclusion, breaking into the mainstream is a complex interplay of radio airplay, press exposure, and strategic marketing. For Neon Frequencies, their journey was marked by both triumphs and challenges, but their unwavering dedication to their craft and their ability to adapt to the ever-changing landscape of the music industry ultimately led to their well-deserved success.

The Roaring 20s: Neon Frequencies Takes Over the Music Scene

As the clock struck midnight on January 1, 2020, the world stood on the brink of a new decade, one that promised innovation, excitement, and a fresh wave of creativity. For the band Neon Frequencies, this moment marked the beginning of their meteoric rise to fame, a journey that would see them transform from local sensations into global superstars. This chapter delves into the pivotal moments and defining characteristics of the Roaring 20s for Neon Frequencies, encapsulating their evolution and the impact they had on the music scene.

The Cultural Climate of the Roaring 20s

The 2020s began amidst a backdrop of social change and technological advancement. Streaming platforms surged in popularity, reshaping how music was consumed and distributed. The advent of social media allowed artists to connect directly with fans, bypassing traditional gatekeepers of the music industry. For Neon Frequencies, these dynamics created an unprecedented opportunity to amplify their reach and influence.

The band capitalized on these trends, leveraging platforms like TikTok and Instagram to share snippets of their music and behind-the-scenes content. Their

THE RISE OF A PHENOMENON

authentic engagement with fans fostered a devoted community that would prove crucial in their rise. The power of viral trends became a tool they wielded skillfully, with one of their tracks becoming a TikTok sensation, leading to an explosion of streams and downloads.

Breaking into the Mainstream

In early 2021, Neon Frequencies released their much-anticipated sophomore album, *Electric Dreams*. The album was a bold departure from their debut, showcasing a matured sound that incorporated elements of electronic, pop, and rock. The lead single, "Chasing Stars," quickly climbed the charts, thanks in part to its infectious melody and relatable lyrics. The song's success was not merely a stroke of luck; it was the result of a meticulously crafted marketing strategy that included targeted ads and collaborations with influential social media personalities.

The equation for success can be modeled as follows:

$$S = f(M, E, C) \qquad (27)$$

Where:

- S = Success of the single
- M = Marketing efforts (ads, social media engagement)
- E = Engagement from fans (shares, likes, comments)
- C = Collaborations with influencers

In this case, Neon Frequencies scored high on all fronts, leading to their breakout moment. The song not only topped charts but also became a staple at parties and events, embedding itself into the cultural zeitgeist of the time.

The Touring Phenomenon

With their newfound fame, Neon Frequencies embarked on a world tour that would solidify their status as a top-tier act. The tour was not just a series of concerts; it was an experience that combined music, art, and technology. Each show featured stunning visual displays, intricate stage designs, and interactive elements that engaged the audience in ways previously unseen.

The band's ability to create a unique concert experience can be expressed with the following relationship:

$$E = f(V, I, A) \tag{28}$$

Where:

- E = Audience experience
- V = Visual elements (lighting, projections)
- I = Interactivity (fan participation, mobile app features)
- A = Artistic expression (performance art, dance)

Their concerts became the talk of the town, with fans eagerly posting their experiences online, further amplifying the band's reach. The combination of electrifying performances and a strong social media presence created a feedback loop that propelled their popularity.

Navigating Challenges and Triumphs

However, the journey was not without its challenges. The pandemic posed significant hurdles, forcing the band to adapt quickly. Live shows were canceled, and the music industry faced unprecedented disruptions. But rather than retreating, Neon Frequencies embraced the challenge, pivoting to virtual concerts and live-streamed events. Their ability to innovate during this period showcased their resilience and commitment to their art.

The equation representing their adaptability can be formulated as:

$$A = g(R, I) \tag{29}$$

Where:

- A = Adaptability of the band
- R = Resourcefulness in overcoming obstacles
- I = Innovative solutions (virtual concerts, online engagement)

By leveraging technology, they not only maintained their fanbase but also attracted new listeners who were exploring music in new and different ways.

Legacy of the Roaring 20s

As the decade progressed, Neon Frequencies solidified their legacy, becoming a symbol of the new music era. Their influence extended beyond their own music, inspiring a wave of new artists who sought to emulate their success. They became known for their genre-blending sound, and their commitment to authenticity resonated with fans worldwide.

In conclusion, the Roaring 20s were not just a period of success for Neon Frequencies; they represented a transformative era in the music industry. The band's ability to adapt, innovate, and engage with their audience set a new standard for what it means to be a modern artist. As they continued to push boundaries and explore new creative territories, Neon Frequencies left an indelible mark on the music scene, ensuring their place in the annals of music history.

The Hit Single that Catapulted Neon Frequencies to Stardom

In the vibrant tapestry of modern music, there are moments when a single track transcends the ordinary, becoming a cultural phenomenon that resonates across borders and generations. For Neon Frequencies, that moment arrived with their electrifying hit single, *"Electric Dreams."* This track not only showcased the band's unique sound but also served as the catalyst that propelled them into the limelight, marking a pivotal point in their career.

The Genesis of "Electric Dreams"

The inception of *"Electric Dreams"* can be traced back to a serendipitous jam session in a dimly lit studio, where the band members, inspired by the pulsating energy of their city, fused elements of electronic music with soulful melodies. The creative process was characterized by a blend of spontaneity and meticulous craftsmanship, as the band sought to encapsulate the essence of their experiences and emotions into a single track.

The songwriting process was a collaborative effort, with each member contributing their unique flair. Dabin, known for her lyrical prowess, penned verses that spoke to the dreams and aspirations of youth, while the band's instrumentalists crafted a soundscape that was both futuristic and nostalgic. The combination of soaring synths, driving basslines, and infectious hooks created a sonic experience that was impossible to ignore.

Theoretical Framework: The Elements of a Hit Single

To understand what makes a hit single like *"Electric Dreams"* resonate with audiences, we can refer to the theory of musical hooks and their psychological impact. A hook is a memorable musical phrase or lyrical line that captures the listener's attention. According to [?], a successful hook often adheres to the following principles:

- **Simplicity:** The hook should be easy to remember and sing along to.

- **Repetition:** Repeated phrases create familiarity, increasing the likelihood of audience retention.

- **Emotional Resonance:** Lyrics that evoke strong emotions can create a deeper connection with listeners.

In *"Electric Dreams,"* the chorus exemplifies these principles, featuring a catchy melody that is both simple and repetitive, while the lyrics evoke a sense of hope and longing, resonating with a wide audience.

Challenges Faced During Production

Despite the initial excitement surrounding *"Electric Dreams,"* the path to its release was not without obstacles. During the production phase, the band faced significant challenges, including creative differences and technical difficulties in the studio. The pressure to deliver a standout track weighed heavily on the members, leading to moments of tension and disagreement.

One notable challenge arose during the mixing process, where the band struggled to balance the electronic elements with organic instrumentation. The equation for achieving the perfect mix can be represented as:

$$M = \frac{E + I}{T} \tag{30}$$

Where: - M = Mix quality - E = Electronic elements - I = Organic instrumentation - T = Technical proficiency

The band's sound engineer, after several iterations, managed to find the ideal balance, resulting in a polished final product that captured the essence of Neon Frequencies.

The Release and Immediate Impact

Upon its release, *"Electric Dreams"* quickly gained traction, climbing the charts and garnering airplay on major radio stations. The track's infectious energy and relatable lyrics resonated with listeners, leading to viral trends on social media platforms. The accompanying music video, featuring stunning visuals and a narrative that mirrored the song's themes, further amplified its reach.

The impact of *"Electric Dreams"* was not only felt in the charts but also in the hearts of fans. The song became an anthem for a generation, encapsulating the spirit of adventure and the pursuit of dreams. It was during this time that Neon Frequencies began to see their fan base grow exponentially, as audiences flocked to their live shows, eager to experience the magic of the band in person.

Awards and Recognition

The success of *"Electric Dreams"* did not go unnoticed within the industry. The single earned the band several accolades, including nominations for prestigious music awards. The recognition served as a testament to their hard work and creativity, solidifying their place in the music landscape.

In conclusion, *"Electric Dreams"* was more than just a hit single; it was a defining moment for Neon Frequencies. The track's infectious energy, emotional resonance, and the band's dedication to their craft combined to create a cultural touchstone that would be remembered for years to come. As they took to the stage to perform this anthem, it was clear that they were no longer just a band; they were a force to be reckoned with in the world of music.

On the Road with Neon Frequencies

On the Road with Neon Frequencies

On the Road with Neon Frequencies

The journey of a band is often defined by the experiences they share while touring. For Neon Frequencies, the road was not just a means to an end; it was an exhilarating adventure that shaped their identity and solidified their bond as a collective. This chapter delves into the excitement, challenges, and transformative moments that define life on the road for Neon Frequencies.

From Local Heroes to Global Superstars

As Neon Frequencies transitioned from local performances to international tours, they encountered a whirlwind of emotions and experiences. The excitement of stepping onto larger stages was palpable, yet it came with its unique set of challenges. The band had to adapt to the rigors of touring life, which often included long hours on the road, varying climates, and the pressure of maintaining their musical integrity while catering to a growing fanbase.

The journey from local heroes to global superstars is illustrated by their meteoric rise in popularity. Their early shows were characterized by intimate venues filled with passionate fans, but soon they found themselves performing in front of thousands, where every note played could echo in the memories of their audience. The transition was not merely a change in scale but a shift in their artistic approach, as they began to experiment with their sound to resonate with a broader audience.

The Excitement and Challenges of Touring

Touring is a double-edged sword. On one side lies the thrill of performing live, the adrenaline rush of connecting with fans, and the joy of sharing music. On the other side, there are the logistical nightmares: travel delays, technical difficulties, and the inevitable fatigue that comes with being on the road for extended periods.

The excitement of touring can be likened to the thrill of a high-speed chase in a blockbuster film. Each concert is a climax, a moment where everything must come together perfectly. However, just as in a movie, the behind-the-scenes struggles often go unnoticed. The band faced challenges such as coordinating schedules, managing equipment, and ensuring that every member was in peak condition to deliver electrifying performances.

Life on the Road: Adventures and Misadventures

Life on the road is a tapestry woven with both adventures and misadventures. From spontaneous detours to hidden gems discovered in unfamiliar cities, Neon Frequencies embraced the unpredictability of touring. Each stop along their journey offered new experiences, from late-night food runs in bustling cities to quiet moments of reflection in hotel rooms.

However, misadventures were just as common. There were times when equipment malfunctioned mid-performance, leading to improvised solutions that showcased the band's resourcefulness. These moments not only tested their resilience but also strengthened their camaraderie, as they learned to lean on one another in times of crisis.

The Bonding and Conflict within the Band

Touring can amplify both the bonds and conflicts within a band. The shared experiences of performing, traveling, and navigating the highs and lows of fame fostered a deep connection among the members of Neon Frequencies. Late-night jam sessions and heartfelt conversations solidified their friendship and creative synergy.

Yet, the close quarters of touring also led to moments of tension. Creative differences emerged as each member sought to assert their artistic vision. Navigating these conflicts required open communication and a willingness to compromise. The band learned that, much like in any successful collaboration, understanding and respecting each other's perspectives was crucial to maintaining harmony.

Late-Night Jam Sessions and Impromptu Collaborations

One of the most cherished aspects of life on the road for Neon Frequencies was the late-night jam sessions. After a long day of travel and performance, the band often found solace in making music together. These impromptu collaborations served as a creative outlet, allowing them to experiment with new ideas and sounds.

The magic of these sessions lay in their spontaneity. With no pressure to perform for an audience, the band could explore uncharted musical territories, leading to the creation of some of their most memorable songs. These moments became a cornerstone of their artistic identity, reinforcing the idea that creativity thrives in an environment of freedom and collaboration.

Conclusion

The road was more than just a backdrop for Neon Frequencies; it was an integral part of their story. The experiences they shared, both exhilarating and challenging, shaped their music and their relationships. As they navigated the complexities of touring, they emerged not only as a band but as a family, united by their passion for music and the unforgettable moments they created together. The road may have been long, but it was filled with the vibrant colors of adventure, growth, and the indelible spirit of Neon Frequencies.

From Local Heroes to Global Superstars

The Excitement and Challenges of Touring

Touring is often regarded as the pinnacle of a musician's career, a thrilling adventure that brings the music to life in front of eager audiences. For Dabin and Neon Frequencies, the excitement of touring was palpable, a rush that came from performing live and connecting with fans on a personal level. This section explores the dual nature of touring, highlighting both the exhilaration and the challenges that accompany life on the road.

The Thrill of Live Performance

Nothing compares to the electric atmosphere of a live concert. The moment the lights dim and the first notes reverberate through the venue, a palpable energy fills the air. For Dabin and her bandmates, this was where their music transformed from recorded tracks into a shared experience. The adrenaline rush of performing in front of thousands of fans is a unique high, often described as euphoric.

$$E = \frac{1}{2}mv^2 \tag{31}$$

where E represents the energy of the performance, m is the mass of the band's collective talent, and v is the velocity of the audience's reaction. The more engaged the audience, the greater the energy, creating a feedback loop that fuels the performance.

The excitement of touring also stems from the diverse locations and cultures that the band encounters. Each city offers a new backdrop, new fans, and unique experiences that enrich the band's journey. The thrill of exploring new places while sharing their music creates an unforgettable tapestry of memories.

The Challenges of Life on the Road

Despite the excitement, touring is not without its challenges. The rigorous schedule can take a toll on the band's physical and mental health. Long hours on buses, late-night performances, and the constant demand for energy can lead to exhaustion.

One of the most significant challenges is the impact of travel on personal relationships. The band members often find themselves away from family and friends for extended periods. This separation can lead to feelings of isolation and homesickness, which, if not addressed, may strain their relationships both within and outside the band.

$$S = \frac{d}{t} \tag{32}$$

where S represents the stress level, d is the distance from home, and t is the time spent away. As the distance increases and time away extends, the stress level can escalate, creating a need for effective coping strategies.

Moreover, the unpredictability of touring can lead to logistical nightmares. From equipment malfunctions to last-minute venue changes, the band must be prepared to adapt. For example, during one tour, a critical piece of equipment failed just hours before a show, forcing the band to quickly improvise. Such challenges test the band's resilience and teamwork, ultimately strengthening their bond.

The Balancing Act

Finding a balance between the excitement of performing and the challenges of touring is crucial for maintaining the band's health and success. Dabin and her bandmates learned to implement strategies to cope with the rigors of life on the road.

Regular communication among band members became essential. They established routines for checking in with each other, both emotionally and logistically. This practice not only helped mitigate stress but also fostered a sense of unity and support.

In addition, prioritizing self-care became a critical component of their touring regimen. The band incorporated practices such as yoga, meditation, and proper nutrition to combat fatigue and maintain their energy levels.

Conclusion

Touring is a double-edged sword, filled with exhilarating highs and daunting challenges. For Dabin and Neon Frequencies, the excitement of connecting with fans and exploring new places was often tempered by the difficulties of life on the road. However, by embracing both the thrill and the challenges, they not only grew as musicians but also as a cohesive unit. The lessons learned during their tours became integral to their identity, shaping their music and their journey in the industry. The road may be long and winding, but for Dabin and her band, it was a journey worth taking.

Life on the Road: Adventures and Misadventures

Life on the road for Neon Frequencies was a whirlwind of excitement, challenges, and unforgettable moments. Each tour stop brought a new adventure, a new city, and a new audience, but it also came with its fair share of misadventures that tested the band's resilience and camaraderie.

The Thrill of Touring

Touring is often romanticized as a glamorous lifestyle filled with bright lights and enthusiastic fans. For Neon Frequencies, the thrill began the moment the tour bus rolled out of their hometown. The anticipation of performing in front of a live audience ignited a fire within each band member. As the adrenaline surged, they would often reminisce about their humble beginnings, reminding themselves of the long journey that brought them to this point.

The excitement was palpable during their first few shows, where the intimate venues allowed them to connect deeply with their fans. Each performance felt like a shared celebration, a moment where music transcended the mundane and brought people together. The band's chemistry on stage was electric, and they thrived on the energy radiating from the audience.

The Challenges of Life on the Road

However, the road was not always smooth. The challenges of touring often overshadowed the glamorous aspects. Long hours on the bus, sleepless nights, and the constant pressure to perform took a toll on the band members' physical and mental health. The demanding schedule left little room for rest, and fatigue became a constant companion.

One notable incident occurred during a particularly grueling stretch of their tour. After a late-night show, the band was scheduled to drive overnight to their next gig. Exhausted, they decided to take turns driving. Unfortunately, fatigue set in for one of the band members, leading to a near-miss accident on a winding road. This close call served as a stark reminder of the dangers of life on the road and the importance of prioritizing safety over ambition.

Adventures in New Cities

Despite the challenges, each city brought new adventures. Exploring local culture and cuisine became a cherished ritual. The band often ventured out to discover hidden gems, from quaint coffee shops to bustling street markets. They made it a point to interact with locals, sharing stories and learning about the places they visited.

In one memorable instance, while touring in New Orleans, the band stumbled upon a vibrant street festival. Drawn in by the lively music and colorful atmosphere, they decided to join in the festivities. This spontaneous decision led to an impromptu jam session with local musicians, creating a fusion of sounds that left both the band and the audience captivated. This experience not only enriched their musical repertoire but also solidified their bond as a group.

Misadventures and Band Dynamics

Misadventures were a common occurrence, often leading to humorous stories that the band would recount for years to come. One such incident involved a miscommunication about their hotel accommodations. After a long drive, the band arrived at what they thought was their hotel, only to discover it was fully booked. In a moment of panic, they scrambled to find alternative lodging, leading to a night spent in a quirky roadside motel.

This experience, while frustrating at the time, became a bonding moment for the band. They laughed through the discomfort, sharing ghost stories and late-night snacks, turning a misadventure into a cherished memory. These moments of levity were crucial in maintaining their camaraderie, especially during the more challenging times.

The Importance of Teamwork

Life on the road also highlighted the importance of teamwork. Each member had a role to play, whether it was managing equipment, coordinating logistics, or keeping spirits high. The dynamic within the band was crucial for navigating the ups and downs of touring life.

For instance, when one member faced personal challenges, the others rallied around to provide support. They created a culture of openness, encouraging each other to share their struggles and celebrate their victories. This camaraderie not only strengthened their bond but also translated into their performances, where their unity shone through on stage.

Conclusion

In conclusion, life on the road for Neon Frequencies was a tapestry woven with threads of adventure and misadventure. The thrill of performing was often tempered by the challenges of touring, but these experiences ultimately shaped the band's identity. Through laughter, camaraderie, and a shared passion for music, they navigated the complexities of life on the road, creating memories that would last a lifetime. As they continued their journey, they embraced each moment, knowing that every adventure, no matter how challenging, was an integral part of their story.

The Bonding and Conflict within the Band

In the exhilarating world of music, the dynamic between band members can often resemble a high-stakes game of chess, where every move can lead to harmony or discord. For Neon Frequencies, the journey was no different. The bond that formed between the members of the band was both a source of creative energy and a potential breeding ground for conflict. Understanding this duality is crucial to appreciating their evolution as artists.

The Foundations of Bonding

At the heart of Neon Frequencies was a shared passion for music. This passion acted as a catalyst for the initial bonding among the band members. As they gathered in dimly lit basements and garages for their early jam sessions, a sense of camaraderie began to flourish. They were not just colleagues; they were friends united by a common goal—creating something extraordinary.

The theory of *social identity* plays a significant role in understanding this bonding process. According to Henri Tajfel's Social Identity Theory, individuals categorize themselves and others into groups, leading to a sense of belonging and shared identity. For Neon Frequencies, being part of a band created a strong in-group identity that fostered loyalty and collaboration. The band members often referred to each other as "family," emphasizing the deep emotional connections that transcended mere professional relationships.

Creative Synergy: The Power of Collaboration

As the band began to write and perform together, their collective creativity blossomed. Each member brought unique talents and perspectives, which, when combined, resulted in a sound that was greater than the sum of its parts. This phenomenon can be explained through *synergistic collaboration*, where the interaction of diverse skills leads to innovative outcomes.

For example, during the creation of their hit single, "Electric Dreams," the band experienced a moment of creative synergy that exemplified this concept. Guitarist Alex introduced a catchy riff, while drummer Mia added a pulsating beat. Meanwhile, lead vocalist Dabin infused the melody with emotive lyrics inspired by personal experiences. The result was a track that resonated with listeners on multiple levels, showcasing the power of collaboration.

Navigating Conflict: The Challenges of Creativity

However, the path to success was not without its challenges. The same creative energy that fueled their music also led to moments of tension and conflict. Disagreements over artistic direction, songwriting credits, and performance styles were common. These conflicts often stemmed from the individual desires of band members to express their unique artistic visions.

One notable incident occurred during the recording of their second album. Dabin envisioned a more experimental sound, while bassist Sam preferred to stick to their established style. This clash of ideas led to heated discussions in the studio, highlighting the delicate balance between collaboration and individual expression.

Such conflicts are not uncommon in creative environments and can be analyzed through the lens of *constructive conflict theory*, which posits that conflict can lead to positive outcomes if managed effectively.

Conflict Resolution: Finding Common Ground

To navigate these conflicts, Neon Frequencies developed a set of strategies that allowed them to maintain their bond while addressing their differences. Open communication became essential. Regular band meetings were held to discuss ideas, grievances, and visions for the future. This practice not only fostered transparency but also ensured that every member felt heard and valued.

Additionally, the band embraced the concept of *collaborative problem-solving*. Instead of viewing conflicts as obstacles, they approached them as opportunities for growth. For instance, during the aforementioned disagreement about the album's direction, they decided to experiment with both styles. The resulting tracks combined elements of their original sound with new influences, ultimately leading to a more diverse and innovative album.

The Role of Trust and Respect

At the core of Neon Frequencies' ability to bond and resolve conflicts was a foundation of trust and mutual respect. Each member recognized the importance of the others' contributions and the value of their unique perspectives. This respect allowed them to navigate the inevitable ups and downs of being in a band without losing sight of their shared goals.

The concept of *trust* in group dynamics can be linked to the work of social psychologist David Schoorman, who identified trust as a critical component of team performance. In the case of Neon Frequencies, trust enabled them to take creative risks and explore new musical territories without fear of judgment or rejection.

Conclusion: A Journey of Growth

In conclusion, the bonding and conflict within Neon Frequencies were integral to their identity as a band. Their shared passion for music fostered deep connections, while the challenges they faced ultimately led to growth and innovation. By embracing both the highs and lows of their journey, they crafted a unique sound that resonated with fans worldwide. The lessons learned from their experiences serve as a testament to the power of collaboration, trust, and the enduring spirit of creativity in the face of adversity.

Through these trials, Neon Frequencies not only solidified their bond but also carved a path for their legacy in the music industry. The interplay of bonding and conflict is a reminder that even in the most harmonious of collaborations, the potential for discord exists, and it is through navigating these challenges that true artistry is born.

Late-Night Jam Sessions and Impromptu Collaborations

The magic of music often occurs in the most unexpected moments, and for Neon Frequencies, late-night jam sessions became the crucible for creativity, innovation, and bonding. These sessions were not just casual gatherings; they were the lifeblood of the band, where ideas flowed as freely as the coffee and inspiration surged like a crescendo in a symphony.

The Atmosphere of Creativity

The ambiance during these late-night sessions was electric. Dim lights, scattered instruments, and an array of snacks created a comfortable yet charged environment. It was here, in the intimate setting of their rehearsal space, that the members of Neon Frequencies could let their guard down and explore the depths of their musical identities. The relaxed atmosphere fostered a sense of freedom, allowing each member to express themselves without the constraints of formal songwriting.

Spontaneity in Collaboration

One of the most thrilling aspects of these jam sessions was the spontaneity they encouraged. Often, a single riff or a simple beat would spark a flurry of ideas. For instance, during one memorable session, Dabin picked up her guitar and began strumming a haunting melody. Almost instantly, the drummer joined in with a syncopated rhythm, and the bassist layered in a groove that felt both familiar and fresh. This organic collaboration led to the creation of what would later become one of their hit tracks, illustrating how the synergy of the band could transform a fleeting moment into a lasting piece of art.

Theoretical Framework of Collaboration

From a theoretical standpoint, the concept of collaboration in music can be analyzed through the lens of social constructivism, which posits that knowledge and meaning are constructed through social interactions. In the context of Neon Frequencies, each member brought their unique experiences and influences, contributing to a collective sound that was greater than the sum of its parts. The band's dynamic can be modeled mathematically as:

$$S = \sum_{i=1}^{n} E_i$$

where S represents the overall sound of the band, E_i represents the individual contributions of each member, and n is the number of band members. This equation emphasizes the importance of each member's input in shaping the band's identity.

Challenges and Resolutions

However, these late-night sessions were not without their challenges. Creative differences occasionally arose, leading to moments of tension. For example, during one session, a disagreement over the direction of a new song led to a heated debate. Dabin favored a more experimental approach, while another band member preferred a traditional structure. To resolve this conflict, they decided to split the difference—creating two versions of the song that showcased both styles. This compromise not only enriched their repertoire but also reinforced the importance of flexibility and open communication within the band.

The Impact on Their Sound

The late-night jam sessions played a pivotal role in the evolution of Neon Frequencies' sound. They allowed the band to experiment with various genres and styles, blending elements of rock, electronic, and even jazz. For instance, one night, inspired by a late-night documentary on jazz legends, the band decided to incorporate improvisational elements into their music. This experimentation led to a unique fusion sound that became a hallmark of their later work.

Memorable Impromptu Collaborations

These sessions also birthed some unforgettable impromptu collaborations. One such instance involved a surprise guest—a local musician who had stopped by to drop off a demo. After a casual introduction, the band invited him to join their jam. The result was an electrifying performance that combined his folk influences with Neon Frequencies' signature sound. This spontaneous collaboration not only enriched their music but also strengthened their ties to the local music community.

Conclusion

In conclusion, the late-night jam sessions and impromptu collaborations of Neon Frequencies were more than just a creative outlet; they were a vital part of the band's identity and growth. These moments of spontaneity and collaboration fostered a unique sound that resonated with fans and critics alike. The ability to come together, share ideas, and push each other creatively was instrumental in shaping their journey and solidifying their place in the music industry. As they moved forward, the spirit of those late-night sessions continued to influence their work, reminding them of the power of collaboration and the magic that can happen when artists unite in the name of creativity.

Behind the Scenes: The Show Must Go On

Rehearsals and Stage Design: Creating a Visual Spectacle

In the world of music, the auditory experience is only part of the equation. To truly captivate an audience, the visual elements of a performance must be equally compelling. For Neon Frequencies, the rehearsals and stage design were not mere logistical necessities; they were the crucibles in which the band's artistic vision was brought to life.

The Importance of Rehearsals

Rehearsals serve as the backbone of any successful performance. They are where the magic begins, allowing band members to hone their craft, synchronize their movements, and refine their sound. A well-structured rehearsal schedule is essential for maximizing productivity and ensuring that every member is on the same page.

Let R represent the total number of rehearsals, and let T be the average duration of each rehearsal in hours. The total rehearsal time H can be expressed mathematically as:

$$H = R \times T$$

For Neon Frequencies, a typical rehearsal consisted of a minimum of three hours, encompassing not only musical practice but also discussions about stage presence, lighting, and overall performance aesthetics.

Stage Design: The Visual Narrative

Stage design is a crucial element that shapes the audience's experience. For Neon Frequencies, the stage was not just a platform; it was a canvas. The design elements included dynamic lighting, intricate backdrops, and innovative props that enhanced the storytelling aspect of their performances.

The design team worked tirelessly to create a visual narrative that complemented the band's music. By employing various lighting techniques, such as moving heads and LED walls, they could evoke emotions that resonated with the songs being performed. The equation for the effectiveness of stage design E can be modeled as:

$$E = L + P + A$$

Where: - L is the quality of lighting, - P is the use of props, - A is the overall atmosphere created.

In the case of Neon Frequencies, their stage design often featured vibrant colors and synchronized light shows that mirrored the tempo and mood of their music.

Challenges in Rehearsals and Design

Despite the excitement surrounding rehearsals and stage design, challenges were inevitable. Technical difficulties, such as equipment failures or miscommunication among band members, could disrupt the flow of rehearsals. Moreover, the creative process often led to disagreements regarding the visual direction of the performance.

For instance, during the preparation for their debut album tour, the band faced a significant challenge when a key piece of lighting equipment malfunctioned just days before a major show. The solution involved a rapid reconfiguration of the stage layout, demonstrating the band's adaptability and commitment to delivering a spectacular performance.

Examples of Successful Integration

One of the most memorable performances by Neon Frequencies was during their sold-out concert at the Grand Arena. The stage design included a massive LED backdrop that displayed mesmerizing visuals, synchronized with the music. This integration of sound and sight created an immersive experience that left the audience in awe.

The rehearsal process leading up to this event was intense. The band spent countless hours perfecting not only their musical arrangements but also the timing of their movements in relation to the lighting cues. The result was a seamless performance that showcased the synergy between the music and the visual spectacle.

Conclusion

In conclusion, the rehearsals and stage design for Neon Frequencies were integral to their identity as a band. By prioritizing both musical precision and visual storytelling, they created performances that transcended mere concerts, transforming them into unforgettable experiences. The meticulous planning and execution of their rehearsals and stage design not only captured the essence of their music but also ensured that every show was a visual feast for their fans. As they continued to evolve, Neon Frequencies remained committed to pushing the boundaries of what a live performance could be, forever striving to create a spectacle that resonated deeply with their audience.

Crafting Setlists to Keep the Energy High

Creating an unforgettable concert experience is not merely about the music; it's an art form that requires careful planning and a deep understanding of audience dynamics. The setlist—the carefully curated list of songs performed during a concert—plays a pivotal role in maintaining high energy levels throughout the performance. This section delves into the theory and practice behind crafting setlists that keep audiences engaged and energized from the opening note to the final encore.

Theoretical Foundations of Setlist Crafting

At its core, a successful setlist is constructed with an understanding of several key principles:

- **Pacing:** Just like a well-crafted narrative, a setlist needs to have its own rhythm. Pacing involves alternating between high-energy songs and slower ballads to create emotional peaks and valleys that keep the audience engaged. This can be illustrated with a simple equation:

$$E(t) = \int_0^T P(t)\, dt \qquad (33)$$

where $E(t)$ represents the energy levels over time, $P(t)$ is the pacing function, and T is the total duration of the performance. A well-balanced setlist will yield a maximized $E(t)$.

- **Audience Engagement:** Understanding the audience's mood and preferences is crucial. This can be measured through audience feedback, ticket sales, and social media interactions. A common approach is to analyze the demographics of the audience and adjust the setlist accordingly to include familiar hits and fan favorites.

- **Dynamic Range:** The dynamic range of a performance refers to the contrast between the loudest and quietest moments. A setlist that includes a variety of tempos and volumes can enhance the emotional impact of the performance. This can be represented by:

$$DR = L_{max} - L_{min} \qquad (34)$$

where DR is the dynamic range, L_{max} is the maximum loudness level, and L_{min} is the minimum loudness level in the setlist.

- **Thematic Cohesion:** A setlist can tell a story or convey a theme. This is particularly important for concept albums or when the band has a distinct artistic vision. Thematic cohesion can be achieved by grouping songs that share lyrical content, musical style, or emotional resonance.

Practical Considerations in Setlist Creation

While the theoretical foundations provide a framework, the practical aspects of setlist creation involve a multitude of factors:

- **Song Selection:** Choosing the right songs is paramount. Bands should consider their most popular tracks, as well as deeper cuts that resonate with dedicated fans. For instance, Neon Frequencies might choose to open with their hit single to immediately capture the audience's attention, followed by a lesser-known track that showcases their musical range.

- **Transitioning:** Smooth transitions between songs can enhance the flow of the performance. This might involve key changes, tempo adjustments, or even spoken interludes that allow the audience to catch their breath before the next energetic number. For example, transitioning from a high-energy anthem to a slower ballad could be achieved by gradually decreasing the tempo and introducing a soft instrumental interlude.

- **Encore Planning:** The encore is a critical component of any setlist. It's the moment when the band leaves the stage and returns for a final performance. This segment should ideally include the band's most beloved songs, ensuring that the audience leaves with a lasting impression. Planning for an encore requires anticipation of audience reaction and energy levels.

- **Feedback Loop:** After each performance, gathering feedback is essential. This can be done through social media, direct audience interaction, or post-concert surveys. Analyzing this feedback can inform future setlist decisions, ensuring that the band evolves with their audience.

Examples of Effective Setlists

To illustrate the principles discussed, let's examine a few examples of effective setlists from renowned bands:

- **The Rolling Stones:** Known for their electrifying performances, the Rolling Stones often open with a high-energy track like *Jumpin' Jack Flash*, followed by a mix of classic hits and newer material, maintaining a balance that keeps the audience on their toes. Their use of dynamic range and pacing is masterful, often culminating in a high-energy finale with *(I Can't Get No) Satisfaction*.

- **Beyoncé:** In her concerts, Beyoncé expertly weaves together themes of empowerment and nostalgia. Her setlists often start with powerful anthems, transition into slower ballads, and then ramp up again for a high-energy climax. The pacing and audience engagement are meticulously crafted to create an unforgettable experience.

- **Coldplay:** Coldplay is known for their emotional storytelling through music. Their setlists often follow a narrative arc, starting with reflective songs and building to euphoric anthems, such as *Viva La Vida* as a show-stopping centerpiece.

Conclusion

Crafting a setlist that keeps the energy high is a blend of art and science. By understanding the theoretical foundations of pacing, audience engagement, dynamic range, and thematic cohesion, while also considering practical elements like song selection, transitions, and audience feedback, bands like Neon Frequencies can create electrifying performances that resonate with fans long after the final note has faded. The magic of live music lies in these carefully curated moments, where every song is a thread in the tapestry of a shared experience, leaving audiences exhilarated and yearning for more.

The Art of Engaging the Audience: Crowd Interaction and Participation

In the realm of live music, the connection between the performers and the audience is often regarded as the heartbeat of a successful concert. Engaging the crowd transforms a mere performance into an unforgettable experience. This section delves into the intricacies of crowd interaction, exploring its theoretical foundations, practical applications, and the challenges artists face in creating a participatory atmosphere.

Theoretical Foundations of Audience Engagement

The theory of audience engagement is rooted in several psychological and sociological concepts. One key framework is the **Social Identity Theory**, which posits that individuals derive a sense of self from their group memberships. In a concert setting, fans identify with the band and fellow attendees, creating a collective identity that enhances their experience. This phenomenon is further amplified by the **Flow Theory**, which suggests that individuals achieve a state of heightened focus and enjoyment when fully immersed in an activity. Musicians can facilitate this state by fostering an environment conducive to participation and connection.

Techniques for Engaging the Audience

1. **Call and Response:** This age-old technique invites the audience to participate actively. By prompting fans to repeat phrases or sounds, artists create a dialogue that energizes the crowd. For instance, during a performance of their hit single, Dabin might lead the audience in a call-and-response segment, eliciting cheers and vocalizations that enhance the overall atmosphere.

2. **Interactive Storytelling:** Musicians can engage their audience by sharing personal anecdotes or the stories behind their songs. This narrative approach not only humanizes the artist but also invites the audience to connect on a deeper level. For example, before performing a poignant ballad, Dabin might recount the

inspiration behind the song, allowing fans to feel a sense of intimacy and shared experience.

3. **Physical Engagement:** Encouraging fans to dance, clap, or move in sync with the music creates a dynamic atmosphere. Dabin's performances often include moments where she invites the audience to wave their hands or jump to the beat, fostering a sense of unity and collective energy.

4. **Utilizing Technology:** In today's digital age, social media and live streaming provide unique opportunities for engagement. Artists can encourage fans to share their experiences online, creating a virtual community that extends beyond the concert venue. For instance, Dabin might invite fans to use a specific hashtag during the show, allowing them to connect and share their excitement in real-time.

Challenges in Audience Engagement

While engaging the audience is essential, it is not without its challenges. One significant issue is the **Diversity of Audience Preferences.** Concertgoers come from various backgrounds, each with unique expectations and tastes. Striking a balance between catering to individual preferences while maintaining a cohesive experience can be daunting. For instance, a heavy electronic track may resonate with some fans, while others may prefer acoustic renditions.

Another challenge is the **Distraction of Technology.** With the prevalence of smartphones, audiences often find themselves more engaged with their devices than the performance itself. Artists must navigate this landscape, finding innovative ways to draw attention back to the stage. Dabin might address this by encouraging fans to put their phones down during specific moments, emphasizing the importance of being present in the experience.

Examples of Successful Audience Engagement

The success of audience engagement can be measured through various metrics, including audience response, social media interaction, and overall concert atmosphere. One notable example is **Beyoncé's Coachella Performance**, where she masterfully engaged the crowd through intricate choreography, call-and-response segments, and emotional storytelling. The result was a performance that resonated deeply with fans, leaving an indelible mark on the cultural landscape.

Similarly, Dabin's performances often exemplify effective audience engagement. During a recent concert, she seamlessly integrated crowd participation by inviting fans to sing along during the chorus of her hit song. The palpable energy created a feedback loop, where the audience's enthusiasm further fueled her performance, resulting in a euphoric atmosphere.

Conclusion

The art of engaging the audience is a multifaceted endeavor that requires a deep understanding of psychological principles, innovative techniques, and the ability to navigate challenges. By fostering crowd interaction and participation, artists like Dabin create memorable experiences that transcend the music itself. The connection forged between performer and audience not only enhances the concert experience but also solidifies the bond between the artist and their fans, ensuring that the echoes of their performances resonate long after the final note fades away.

From Small Venues to Stadiums: The Evolution of their Live Performances

As Neon Frequencies ascended from local heroes to global superstars, their live performances transformed dramatically, mirroring their growth and the evolution of their sound. The journey began in intimate settings where the energy was palpable, and each note resonated deeply with a handful of devoted fans. These small venues, often characterized by their close-knit atmosphere, allowed for a raw and authentic connection between the band and their audience. The early performances were marked by an experimental spirit, where each show was a unique exploration of sound and emotion.

The Intimacy of Small Venues

In the early days, Neon Frequencies played in cozy clubs and small theaters, where the audience was often just a few feet away from the stage. This proximity fostered an intimate environment, enabling the band to experiment with their setlists and engage directly with fans. The feedback loop was immediate; cheers, claps, and even the occasional shout of encouragement from the crowd fueled their performances.

The challenges of small venues were numerous, including limited space and sound equipment. However, these constraints often led to creative solutions. For example, the band would occasionally forgo elaborate lighting setups in favor of acoustic renditions of their songs, allowing the raw talent of each member to shine through. This period was foundational, as it shaped their identity and honed their performance skills.

Transitioning to Larger Venues

As their popularity surged, Neon Frequencies began to transition to larger venues. This shift was not merely about scaling up; it involved a complete rethinking of their performance dynamics. Larger venues required a more structured approach to set design, sound engineering, and audience engagement. The intimate connection they had fostered in small venues had to evolve into a more theatrical presentation.

$$E = \frac{P}{A} \tag{35}$$

where E is the energy perceived by the audience, P is the performance intensity, and A is the area of the venue. As the area A increased, the band had to amplify their performance intensity P to maintain the same level of audience engagement E.

The introduction of professional sound systems and stage designs allowed Neon Frequencies to craft a more immersive experience. They began to incorporate visual elements such as dynamic lighting, video projections, and elaborate stage setups. These enhancements were not just aesthetic; they served to elevate the overall performance and create a spectacle that resonated with larger audiences.

The Stadium Experience

The pinnacle of their evolution came when Neon Frequencies played in stadiums, where they faced the ultimate challenge of engaging thousands of fans. Here, the stakes were higher, and the need for a captivating performance was paramount. The band embraced this challenge by developing a multi-sensory experience that went beyond just music.

To maintain the energy and connection with the audience, they employed several strategies:

- **Visual Storytelling**: Each song was accompanied by visuals that complemented the lyrics and themes, creating a narrative that drew the audience into the experience.

- **Audience Interaction**: They utilized technology, such as mobile apps, to engage fans during performances, allowing them to participate in polls or request songs in real-time.

- **Guest Appearances**: Collaborating with other artists during stadium shows added an element of surprise and excitement, drawing in diverse fan bases and enhancing the overall atmosphere.

The culmination of these efforts was evident in their landmark stadium performances, which not only showcased their musical prowess but also their ability to create unforgettable experiences. Each concert became a unique event, a celebration of their journey, and a testament to their evolution.

Challenges and Triumphs

Despite the glamour of stadium performances, the transition was fraught with challenges. The technical demands increased, and the pressure to deliver flawless shows was immense. Issues such as sound delays, equipment failures, and the need for precise choreography became part of the reality of large-scale performances.

However, these challenges also spurred innovation. For instance, the band invested in advanced sound technology to minimize delays, ensuring that the audience experienced the music as intended. They also embraced rehearsal techniques that emphasized synchronization and timing, crucial for maintaining the flow of their performances.

In conclusion, the evolution of Neon Frequencies from small venues to stadiums encapsulates their growth as artists and performers. Each stage of their journey contributed to their identity, shaping not only their music but also their connection with fans. As they continue to push the boundaries of live performance, they remain committed to delivering experiences that resonate deeply with audiences, regardless of the size of the venue. The journey is ongoing, and with each performance, Neon Frequencies redefines what it means to be a live band in the modern music landscape.

The Neon Frequencies Fan Experience

The Devoted Fanbase: From Fanatics to Fandom

In the ever-evolving landscape of the music industry, the relationship between artists and their fans has transformed dramatically. For Neon Frequencies, this transformation is not just a phenomenon; it is a powerful narrative that underscores the band's journey from local sensations to global superstars. The devoted fanbase of Neon Frequencies epitomizes the transition from mere fanatics to a vibrant, engaged fandom, creating a unique cultural ecosystem around the band.

The Psychology of Fandom

At the heart of this devoted fanbase lies a complex psychology that drives individuals to form deep connections with the music and the artists behind it. According to social identity theory, individuals often derive part of their identity from their affiliation with groups, including fandoms. This identification fosters a sense of belonging, community, and shared purpose among fans.

$$S = \frac{B + C}{N} \tag{36}$$

Where:

- S = Sense of belonging
- B = Bonds formed within the group
- C = Collective identity shared among members
- N = Number of group members

As Neon Frequencies' music resonated with listeners, fans began to forge bonds through shared experiences, whether at concerts, online discussions, or fan events. The band's ability to articulate feelings of love, loss, and hope allowed fans to see reflections of their own lives in the lyrics, deepening their emotional investment.

From Local Heroes to Global Icons

The grassroots efforts of Neon Frequencies to connect with their audience laid the foundation for a robust fanbase. Early on, the band engaged with fans through intimate performances at local venues, where the energy was palpable, and the connection was personal. These initial interactions created a loyal following, as fans felt a sense of ownership over the band's success.

As the band began to gain traction, their local following rapidly expanded. The power of word-of-mouth marketing became evident as fans shared their experiences on social media platforms, amplifying the band's reach. This organic growth was further fueled by the band's commitment to authenticity and vulnerability in their music, allowing fans to feel like they were part of the band's journey.

The Role of Social Media

In today's digital age, social media serves as a powerful tool for artists to connect with their fans. Neon Frequencies harnessed platforms such as Instagram, Twitter,

THE NEON FREQUENCIES FAN EXPERIENCE

and TikTok to share behind-the-scenes glimpses, engage in real-time conversations, and foster a sense of community. The band's social media presence allowed fans to interact directly with the members, blurring the lines between celebrity and everyday life.

The phenomenon of "fan art" and "fan fiction" emerged as fans expressed their creativity and devotion. This not only solidified their connection to the band but also contributed to a larger narrative that fans could participate in. The hashtag campaigns initiated by the band further encouraged fan interaction, creating a shared language and culture within the fandom.

The Evolution of Fan Culture

As Neon Frequencies' popularity surged, so did the complexity of their fan culture. The transition from fanatics to fandom involved the establishment of fan clubs, online forums, and even conventions dedicated to celebrating the band's music. This evolution marked a significant shift in how fans interacted with each other and the band itself.

$$F_c = \sum_{i=1}^{N}(E_i + C_i + I_i) \tag{37}$$

Where:

- F_c = Fandom culture
- E_i = Engagement activities (meet-ups, concerts)
- C_i = Collaborative projects (fan art, covers)
- I_i = Interaction with the band (social media, Q&As)

The dedicated fanbase of Neon Frequencies not only consumed the band's music but actively participated in its creation and dissemination. This collaborative spirit fostered a sense of agency among fans, further solidifying their commitment to the band.

Challenges and Triumphs

However, the journey from fanatics to fandom is not without its challenges. As the band rose to fame, the dynamics within the fanbase began to shift. The pressures of celebrity culture, coupled with the expectations placed on the band, led to moments of tension and conflict among fans. Differing opinions on artistic direction or personal choices made by band members occasionally sparked debates within the community.

Despite these challenges, the resilience of the Neon Frequencies fandom shone through. Fans rallied together during tough times, supporting each other and the band through social media campaigns and fundraising efforts for mental health awareness. This solidarity not only reinforced their bond but also highlighted the positive impact of fandom on individual well-being.

Conclusion

In conclusion, the devoted fanbase of Neon Frequencies exemplifies the profound connection between artists and their audience. From local heroes to global icons, the band's journey is intricately linked to the evolution of their fandom. Through shared experiences, social media engagement, and a collaborative spirit, fans have transformed from mere admirers into an integral part of the Neon Frequencies narrative. As the band continues to evolve, the devotion and passion of their fanbase will undoubtedly remain a driving force in their success story, illustrating the timeless power of music to unite and inspire.

Up Close and Personal: Meet and Greets and Fan Events

In the electrifying world of music, where sound meets spectacle, the connection between artists and their fans transcends the auditory experience, creating moments that resonate in the hearts and minds of both parties. For Neon Frequencies, these moments are encapsulated in the intimate settings of meet and greets and fan events, where the boundary between performer and audience dissolves, allowing for a unique exchange of energy and emotion.

The Essence of Connection

At the core of meet and greets lies the fundamental human desire for connection. These events serve as a bridge, enabling fans to interact with Dabin and her bandmates in a setting that feels personal and exclusive. The excitement is palpable as fans gather, their hearts racing with anticipation. The atmosphere is charged, a blend of nervous energy and sheer joy, as they prepare to meet the artists whose music has shaped their lives.

Consider the psychological theory of *social presence*, which posits that the more real and present an individual feels in an interaction, the more meaningful the experience becomes. In this context, meet and greets allow fans to engage with

Dabin not just as a performer, but as a person. This interaction fosters a sense of belonging and community among fans, reinforcing their loyalty to the band.

Planning the Event

Organizing a successful meet and greet involves meticulous planning. Factors such as venue selection, timing, and crowd management play crucial roles in ensuring a smooth experience. For example, choosing a location that is accessible and comfortable enhances the overall atmosphere, while scheduling the event at a time that does not conflict with other activities maximizes attendance.

Moreover, the logistics of managing fan interactions are essential. A common problem faced during such events is the potential for overwhelming crowds. To mitigate this, organizers often implement a ticketing system, allowing fans to reserve their spots in advance. This not only streamlines the process but also creates a sense of exclusivity, making the event feel more special.

Engagement Strategies

Once the event is underway, engagement strategies become paramount. Dabin and her bandmates often employ various techniques to connect with fans on a personal level. For instance, they might initiate conversations by asking fans about their favorite songs or memorable concert experiences. This not only breaks the ice but also makes fans feel valued and heard.

A notable example of this occurred during a meet and greet in Los Angeles, where Dabin took the time to learn the names of each fan present. This simple act of recognition transformed the interaction, as fans left feeling personally acknowledged rather than just another face in the crowd. Such moments are often shared on social media, amplifying the band's connection with their fanbase and encouraging others to participate in future events.

The Impact of Social Media

In the digital age, social media plays a pivotal role in enhancing the meet and greet experience. Platforms such as Instagram and Twitter allow fans to share their experiences in real-time, creating a virtual community that extends beyond the physical event. This phenomenon can be explained through the *social media engagement theory*, which suggests that interactions on social media can deepen relationships and foster a sense of community.

For Neon Frequencies, the impact of social media is evident. Fans often post pictures, videos, and testimonials from meet and greets, generating buzz and excitement for upcoming events. This not only strengthens the band's brand but also serves as a powerful marketing tool, attracting new fans who are eager to join the community.

Fan Events: A Celebration of Community

In addition to meet and greets, Neon Frequencies frequently hosts fan events that celebrate their music and community. These gatherings may include listening parties, album signings, or even themed events that allow fans to immerse themselves in the band's world. Such events create a festive atmosphere, encouraging fans to share their passion for the music and connect with fellow enthusiasts.

An example of this occurred during the launch of their debut album, where a listening party was organized in a local venue. Fans were invited to experience the album in its entirety before its official release, creating a sense of exclusivity and excitement. The event featured live performances, Q&A sessions, and interactive activities, allowing fans to engage with the band in various ways.

The success of these events can be quantified through engagement metrics, such as attendance numbers, social media interactions, and fan feedback. These metrics provide valuable insights into the effectiveness of the events and guide future planning.

Challenges and Considerations

Despite the many benefits of meet and greets and fan events, challenges can arise. One common issue is managing expectations. Fans often arrive with high hopes for a personal interaction, and if the event does not meet those expectations, disappointment can ensue. To address this, clear communication regarding the nature of the event is essential. Setting realistic expectations helps mitigate potential dissatisfaction.

Additionally, the emotional toll on artists must be considered. While Dabin and her bandmates cherish the opportunity to connect with fans, the pressure of constant engagement can lead to burnout. Balancing personal time with public appearances is crucial for maintaining the artists' well-being and ensuring that they can continue to deliver authentic experiences.

Conclusion

Ultimately, meet and greets and fan events are more than mere promotional activities; they are vital components of the Neon Frequencies experience. These interactions foster a sense of community, strengthen bonds between artists and fans, and create lasting memories that resonate long after the music fades. As Dabin and her band continue to evolve, their commitment to connecting with their fans remains unwavering, ensuring that the spirit of Neon Frequencies lives on in the hearts of those who have embraced their music.

The Power of Social Media: Connecting with Fans Worldwide

In the digital age, social media has emerged as a revolutionary platform that has transformed the way artists and bands connect with their fans. For Neon Frequencies, this connection has been pivotal in building a global fanbase and fostering a community that transcends geographical boundaries.

The rise of platforms such as Instagram, Twitter, Facebook, and TikTok has allowed musicians to share their creative processes, personal stories, and live performances in real-time. This immediacy creates a sense of intimacy and accessibility that traditional media could not achieve. According to a study by Smith (2021), approximately 80% of musicians reported that social media significantly enhanced their relationship with fans, allowing for direct engagement and feedback.

Engagement and Interaction

The essence of social media lies in its ability to facilitate two-way communication. Neon Frequencies has harnessed this power by actively engaging with their audience through comments, live Q&A sessions, and interactive posts. This engagement fosters a sense of belonging among fans, as they feel their voices are heard and valued.

For instance, during the release of their hit single, Neon Frequencies initiated a hashtag campaign, #NeonMoments, encouraging fans to share their experiences with the band's music. The campaign went viral, generating thousands of posts and further solidifying the band's connection with their audience.

Content Creation and Sharing

Social media also enables the rapid dissemination of content, allowing Neon Frequencies to share behind-the-scenes footage, rehearsal clips, and personal anecdotes. This content not only humanizes the band but also keeps fans engaged and invested in their journey.

The mathematical model of engagement can be represented as:

$$E = \frac{C \times I}{T}$$

where:

- E = Engagement level
- C = Quality of content shared
- I = Interactivity of posts
- T = Time since last interaction

Higher quality content and interactivity lead to increased engagement, as evidenced by the band's significant follower growth during their active posting periods.

Challenges of Social Media Engagement

Despite its advantages, the use of social media is not without challenges. The constant pressure to maintain an online presence can lead to burnout among band members. Additionally, negative comments and online trolling can impact mental health and the overall morale of the group.

A study by Johnson et al. (2022) indicates that 60% of artists experience anxiety related to their online persona, which can detract from their creative output. Neon Frequencies has addressed this issue by establishing guidelines for social media use, emphasizing the importance of mental health and encouraging breaks from online engagement when necessary.

Global Reach and Cultural Exchange

One of the most remarkable aspects of social media is its ability to connect artists with fans from diverse cultural backgrounds. Neon Frequencies has embraced this global reach by collaborating with international artists and sharing music that reflects various cultural influences.

For example, their collaboration with Brazilian artist Ana Costa on the track "Rhythms of the World" not only showcased their versatility but also introduced their music to new audiences. The success of this collaboration can be analyzed through the following equation:

$$S = \frac{R \times A}{C}$$

where:

- S = Success of collaboration
- R = Reach of both artists
- A = Audience engagement
- C = Cultural barriers

As cultural barriers diminish through social media, artists like Neon Frequencies can create music that resonates with a broader audience, ultimately enriching their artistic expression.

The Future of Fan Interaction

Looking ahead, the role of social media in music will continue to evolve. Innovations such as virtual reality concerts and augmented reality experiences are on the horizon, promising even more immersive ways for fans to connect with their favorite artists. Neon Frequencies is already exploring these technologies to enhance their live performances and fan interactions.

In conclusion, the power of social media has reshaped the landscape of music, providing Neon Frequencies with unparalleled opportunities to connect with fans worldwide. By embracing this digital revolution, the band has not only expanded its reach but has also fostered a vibrant community that celebrates their music and journey together. As they continue to navigate the complexities of the music industry, the influence of social media will undoubtedly remain a cornerstone of their success.

Fan Culture: Tattoos, Memorabilia, and Fan Art

The phenomenon of fan culture surrounding Neon Frequencies transcends mere admiration; it embodies a community deeply invested in the band's identity and legacy. This section explores the vibrant expressions of fandom through tattoos, memorabilia, and fan art, illustrating how these elements create a rich tapestry of connection between the band and its followers.

Tattoos: The Permanent Tribute

One of the most intimate forms of fandom is the tattoo. For many fans, getting a tattoo inspired by Neon Frequencies is akin to wearing their hearts on their sleeves—literally. Tattoos can serve as a lifelong reminder of the connection fans feel to the music and the messages conveyed through the band's lyrics.

$$T = f(M, I, P) \tag{38}$$

Where:

- T = Tattoo significance
- M = Meaning derived from the music
- I = Individual interpretation of the band's themes
- P = Personal experiences tied to the band's influence

For example, a fan may choose to tattoo a lyric that resonated during a pivotal moment in their life, thus creating a personal narrative intertwined with the band's journey. The permanence of tattoos signifies commitment, often fostering a sense of belonging within the broader community of fans who share similar stories.

Memorabilia: Collecting a Piece of History

Memorabilia serves as tangible connections to the band's history, allowing fans to own a piece of the Neon Frequencies legacy. From concert tickets to signed albums, the act of collecting memorabilia can be seen as a form of archiving personal experiences and shared moments.

The value of memorabilia can often be expressed through the following equation:

$$V = R + E + C \tag{39}$$

Where:

- V = Value of the memorabilia
- R = Rarity of the item
- E = Emotional significance to the owner
- C = Cultural relevance within the fan community

Fans often seek out limited edition merchandise, such as vinyl records, exclusive concert posters, and apparel, which not only serve as collectibles but also as symbols of loyalty and dedication. The thrill of owning a piece of Neon Frequencies history can lead to a sense of pride and identity among fans, further solidifying their place within the fandom.

Fan Art: Creative Expressions of Affection

Fan art is another powerful manifestation of admiration for Neon Frequencies. Artists within the fan community create pieces that interpret the band's music, aesthetics, and ethos through various mediums, including painting, digital art, and sculpture. This creative outlet allows fans to express their feelings and interpretations of the band's work, contributing to a broader cultural dialogue.

The relationship between fan art and the band's influence can be conceptualized as:

$$C = A \times I \qquad (40)$$

Where:

- C = Cultural impact of fan art
- A = Artistic expression of the fans
- I = Influence of the band's music and identity

For instance, a fan artist might create a series of illustrations inspired by the themes of love and loss found in Neon Frequencies' songs. These artworks not only resonate with other fans but also serve as a bridge connecting the band's artistic vision with personal interpretations, fostering a sense of community and shared experience.

The Collective Experience

The intersection of tattoos, memorabilia, and fan art encapsulates the essence of fan culture surrounding Neon Frequencies. Each element contributes to a collective experience that transcends individual fandom, creating a vibrant community united by shared passions and experiences.

In essence, fan culture is not merely about admiration; it is an active engagement with the band's narrative, a celebration of creativity, and a testament to the emotional impact of music. As fans continue to express their devotion through these mediums, they not only honor Neon Frequencies but also shape the band's legacy in profound and lasting ways.

Conclusion

The culture surrounding Neon Frequencies is a vivid tapestry woven from the threads of tattoos, memorabilia, and fan art. Each piece of this culture tells a story, reflecting the deep connections fans forge with the music and with each other. As

Neon Frequencies continues to evolve, so too will the expressions of its fanbase, ensuring that the band's legacy remains alive and vibrant for generations to come.

The Rockstar Lifestyle: Parties and Pitfalls

The Glamor and Excesses of the Music Industry

The music industry has long been synonymous with glamor and excess, a world where the bright lights of fame cast long shadows. For many artists, the allure of success is intoxicating, drawing them into a lifestyle filled with luxury, parties, and adoration. However, beneath the surface of this glitzy facade lies a complex web of challenges that can lead to both personal and professional turmoil.

The Illusion of Fame

Fame, often perceived as the ultimate goal for musicians, can create an illusion of happiness and fulfillment. The bright lights of the stage, the roar of the crowd, and the financial rewards can be overwhelmingly enticing. However, this perception often masks the reality of long hours, intense pressure, and the constant scrutiny of public life. As Dabin and Neon Frequencies navigated their rise to stardom, they experienced firsthand the duality of fame—where the highs are exhilarating, but the lows can be devastating.

$$F = \frac{m \cdot a}{v} \qquad (41)$$

Where F represents the force of fame, m is the mass of expectations, a is the acceleration of public interest, and v is the velocity of personal growth. This equation illustrates the pressure that artists face as they try to balance their careers with their personal lives.

The Party Lifestyle

The music industry is often characterized by a culture of celebration, where parties and events are commonplace. These gatherings can serve as networking opportunities, but they also promote a lifestyle that can spiral out of control. For many artists, the temptation to indulge in alcohol, drugs, and other vices can be overwhelming. The party lifestyle, while glamorous, can lead to addiction and mental health struggles.

Dabin's journey was no exception. As the band gained popularity, they found themselves in a whirlwind of parties, late-night celebrations, and the ever-present temptation to celebrate their success. While these moments can be exhilarating, they also come with consequences. The pressure to maintain a certain image and the fear of missing out can lead to a cycle of excess that is difficult to escape.

The Cost of Excess

The cost of living a life filled with excess can be substantial. Financially, artists may find themselves spending lavishly on clothes, cars, and extravagant lifestyles, often leading to unsustainable debt. Emotionally, the toll can be even greater, with many artists facing burnout, anxiety, and depression as they grapple with the demands of their careers and the pitfalls of fame.

Neon Frequencies faced these challenges head-on. As they toured extensively, the band members had to confront the reality of their lifestyle choices. The pressures of fame led to moments of conflict within the group, as differing views on partying and personal responsibility emerged. The balance between enjoying their success and maintaining their health became a crucial topic of discussion.

The Role of Management and Industry Pressure

Management and record labels play a significant role in shaping the lives of artists. The pressure to conform to industry standards and expectations can lead to a culture of excess. Managers often encourage artists to engage in promotional activities that involve partying and socializing, blurring the lines between professional obligations and personal choices.

For Dabin and the members of Neon Frequencies, the influence of management was palpable. They found themselves torn between the desire to enjoy their success and the need to stay grounded. The pressure to maintain a certain public persona often clashed with their personal values, leading to moments of introspection and reevaluation.

Navigating the Glamorous Trap

To navigate the glamor and excess of the music industry, artists must develop a strong sense of self-awareness and resilience. Establishing boundaries, prioritizing mental health, and surrounding themselves with supportive individuals can help mitigate the negative effects of fame. Dabin's journey included moments of reflection where she learned to distinguish between the fleeting allure of excess and the lasting joy of authentic connections.

$$R = \frac{C}{P} \qquad (42)$$

Where R is resilience, C represents the capacity for self-care, and P is the pressure exerted by the industry. This equation emphasizes the importance of maintaining personal well-being in the face of external demands.

Conclusion

In conclusion, while the glamor and excess of the music industry can be alluring, it is essential for artists to recognize the potential pitfalls that accompany fame. Dabin and Neon Frequencies' experience serves as a reminder that success is not solely defined by wealth and recognition, but also by the ability to navigate the complexities of life in the spotlight. By prioritizing mental health, establishing boundaries, and fostering genuine connections, artists can find a balance that allows them to thrive both personally and professionally in an industry often marked by excess.

Balancing Work and Play: The Fine Line

In the exhilarating world of music, where creativity and chaos often intertwine, finding a balance between work and play becomes not just a necessity, but an art form. For the members of Neon Frequencies, this balancing act is akin to walking a tightrope suspended over the roaring crowd of fans and flashing lights. The fine line between maintaining professionalism and indulging in the rockstar lifestyle can often blur, leading to both exhilarating highs and perilous lows.

The Duality of Life on Tour

Touring is a double-edged sword. On one side, it offers the thrill of live performances, the adrenaline rush of connecting with fans, and the joy of sharing music on a grand scale. On the other side, it presents challenges that can strain personal relationships and mental health. The excitement of performing can lead to late-night celebrations and an abundance of socializing, which, while enjoyable, can also detract from the focus required for the band's success.

$$E = \frac{1}{2}mv^2 \qquad (43)$$

In this equation, E represents the energy expended during performances, where m is the mass of the band's collective effort and v is the velocity of their rising fame.

THE ROCKSTAR LIFESTYLE: PARTIES AND PITFALLS

As energy levels peak during the exhilarating moments on stage, the aftermath often requires recovery and reflection, underscoring the need for balance.

Challenges of Excess

The allure of the rockstar lifestyle often brings with it temptations that can lead to excess. Parties, alcohol, and the pressure to maintain a certain image can create a culture of indulgence. For Neon Frequencies, navigating these temptations required a conscious effort to prioritize their health and well-being.

Example: The After-Party Dilemma

Consider a typical scenario after a high-energy concert: the band is invited to an exclusive after-party. The atmosphere is electric, filled with fellow musicians, industry executives, and enthusiastic fans. While the allure of celebration is strong, the consequences of a night of excess can manifest in various ways:

- *Physical Exhaustion:* Late nights can lead to fatigue, affecting vocal performance and overall energy levels for subsequent shows.

- *Mental Health Strain:* The pressure to socialize and maintain a party persona can lead to anxiety and burnout.

- *Relationship Tensions:* Time spent partying can detract from quality time with bandmates, leading to misunderstandings and conflicts.

To combat these challenges, the band adopted strategies that allowed them to enjoy the fruits of their labor without sacrificing their professional integrity.

Strategies for Balance

1. **Scheduled Downtime:** The band learned the importance of scheduling downtime amidst their busy tour schedules. This included designated rest days where they could recharge away from the spotlight.

2. **Mindfulness Practices:** Incorporating mindfulness and meditation helped members manage stress and maintain focus. Techniques such as deep breathing and visualization were employed to ground themselves before performances.

3. **Support Systems:** Establishing a strong support system, both within the band and through trusted friends and family, provided a safety net during challenging times. Open communication about struggles and successes fostered a sense of camaraderie and understanding.

4. **Setting Boundaries:** The band set clear boundaries regarding their social engagements. They learned to say no to certain invitations, prioritizing their health and well-being over fleeting moments of indulgence.

The Consequences of Imbalance

Neglecting the balance between work and play can lead to significant consequences. The pressures of fame can manifest in various ways, including:

- *Substance Abuse:* The temptation to escape the pressures of the music industry can lead to substance abuse, which not only affects the individual but can also jeopardize the band's cohesion.

- *Creative Burnout:* Continuous partying can drain creative energy, leading to a lack of inspiration and diminished performance quality.

- *Public Relations Issues:* Negative press can arise from excessive partying, impacting the band's reputation and fan base.

Conclusion

Ultimately, the journey of Neon Frequencies serves as a reminder that while the rockstar lifestyle is enticing, maintaining a balance between work and play is essential for long-term success. By consciously navigating the challenges and embracing healthy practices, the band not only preserved their artistry but also strengthened their bonds, ensuring that their music continued to resonate with fans around the world. The fine line they tread is a testament to their dedication, resilience, and passion for their craft, proving that even in the whirlwind of fame, it is possible to find harmony amidst the chaos.

Love and Heartbreak: Relationships on the Road

The life of a touring musician is often a whirlwind of excitement, creativity, and, unfortunately, emotional turbulence. Relationships, whether romantic or platonic, are tested under the pressures of constant travel, long hours, and the unique lifestyle that comes with being in a band like Neon Frequencies. In this section, we explore the complexities of love and heartbreak that often accompany life on the road.

The Allure of Romance on Tour

Touring can create an intoxicating environment where connections are forged quickly. The adrenaline of performing, the late-night parties, and the shared experiences can lead to passionate romances. Musicians often find themselves drawn to fans, fellow artists, or even crew members, creating a tapestry of relationships that can be as fleeting as they are intense.

For example, during their early tours, Dabin found herself caught up in a whirlwind romance with a fellow musician from a supporting act. The chemistry was palpable, and their collaboration on stage translated into a deep personal connection. However, the very nature of touring—being constantly on the move—made it difficult for the relationship to flourish outside the confines of the tour bus and the concert venue.

The Challenges of Long-Distance Love

As the band gained popularity, the demands of their schedule intensified. Long stretches away from home meant that maintaining relationships became increasingly difficult. The romantic ideal of being a "rockstar" often clashed with the reality of loneliness and longing.

Consider the case of Dabin and her partner, who struggled to balance their commitments. The equation of time spent together versus time apart can be represented as:

$$R = \frac{T_c}{T_t}$$

where R is the relationship strength, T_c is the time spent together, and T_t is the total time of the relationship. As the band's tour dates multiplied, T_c diminished, leading to a decline in R.

This imbalance often resulted in misunderstandings and feelings of neglect, as partners at home grappled with their own loneliness while trying to support Dabin's burgeoning career. The emotional toll of this lifestyle can be profound, leading to conflicts that might seem trivial in the light of day but become magnified in the isolation of the road.

Heartbreak and Its Aftermath

Heartbreak is an inevitable part of the touring musician's life. As relationships falter, the fallout can be messy. Dabin experienced this firsthand when her relationship ended abruptly after a particularly grueling tour. The emotional distress affected her performances, leading to a cycle of frustration and sadness.

The psychological impact of heartbreak can be understood through the lens of Maslow's hierarchy of needs, where love and belonging are crucial for emotional well-being. When these needs are unmet, musicians may experience a decline in their mental health, which can affect their creativity and performance.

$$E = f(L, B)$$

where E represents emotional health, L represents love, and B represents belonging. As love diminishes, emotional health can spiral downwards, impacting not just personal life but also professional endeavors.

Coping Mechanisms and Healing

In the wake of heartbreak, musicians often turn to their art as a form of catharsis. Dabin channeled her pain into songwriting, creating some of the most poignant tracks in Neon Frequencies' repertoire. This process not only helped her heal but also resonated with fans who could relate to the themes of love and loss.

The band also found solace in their camaraderie. Late-night jam sessions became a therapeutic outlet, allowing members to share their experiences and support each other through their struggles. The shared experience of heartbreak fostered a deeper bond among bandmates, highlighting the importance of community in navigating the emotional rollercoaster of life on the road.

The Cycle of Love and Loss

Ultimately, relationships on the road are characterized by a cycle of love, heartbreak, and healing. Musicians like Dabin learn to navigate these turbulent waters, often emerging stronger and more resilient. Each experience, whether joyful or painful, contributes to their growth as artists and individuals.

As Neon Frequencies continues to evolve, the lessons learned from love and heartbreak remain integral to their journey. These experiences not only shape their music but also enrich their lives, reminding them of the beauty and fragility of human connection in the fast-paced world of touring.

In conclusion, the relationships formed and lost on the road are a testament to the highs and lows of a musician's life. They serve as a reminder that while the music may be the heart of Neon Frequencies, it is the love and heartbreak that truly give it depth and meaning.

The Highs and Lows of Fame

Creative Differences: Navigating Band Dynamics

In the world of music, the chemistry between band members can be as volatile as it is vital. The creative process is often a double-edged sword, where differing opinions and artistic visions collide, leading to both innovation and conflict. For Neon Frequencies, navigating these creative differences was a journey fraught with challenges, yet it ultimately contributed to their dynamic sound and evolution as a band.

The Nature of Creative Differences

Creative differences arise when individual members bring their unique perspectives, influences, and artistic goals to the table. This diversity can lead to rich collaboration but can also result in friction. As noted by [?], creativity thrives in environments that encourage diverse viewpoints, yet it can be stifled when disagreements escalate into personal conflicts. For Neon Frequencies, the band's initial formation saw a blend of varied musical backgrounds, which, while enriching, also set the stage for potential discord.

Theoretical Framework

To understand the dynamics at play, we can apply the **Tuckman's stages of group development**, which outlines the phases teams typically go through: forming, storming, norming, and performing. In the context of Neon Frequencies:

- **Forming:** The band members initially came together, excited and eager to create music. This stage was characterized by high optimism and tentative collaboration.
- **Storming:** As they began to write and perform, differences in musical direction and creative input surfaced. This stage often leads to conflict, as members assert their ideas and preferences.
- **Norming:** Through open communication and compromise, the band gradually learned to appreciate each other's strengths, leading to more cohesive songwriting sessions.
- **Performing:** Ultimately, the band reached a point where they could effectively collaborate, leveraging their differences to enhance their sound.

Examples of Conflict

One notable instance of creative differences occurred during the production of their second album. Dabin, known for her experimental sound, pushed for a more avant-garde approach, incorporating elements of electronic and world music. Meanwhile, other band members favored a more traditional rock sound, leading to heated discussions in the studio.

This tension culminated in a pivotal moment during a recording session. The band had been wrestling with the arrangement of a particular track. Dabin envisioned a complex layering of sounds, while the guitarist advocated for a simpler, more straightforward approach. The disagreement escalated to the point where both parties were frustrated, leading to a temporary halt in recording.

Navigating the Conflict

To resolve this conflict, the band turned to a structured approach to decision-making. They implemented a system where each member could present their ideas and reasoning, followed by a group discussion to evaluate the merits of each proposal. This process encouraged open dialogue and mutual respect, allowing them to navigate their creative differences more effectively.

$$\text{Decision Quality} = f(\text{Diversity of Ideas, Communication Quality, Group Cohesion}) \tag{44}$$

This equation illustrates that the quality of decisions made within the band is a function of the diversity of ideas presented, the quality of communication among members, and the overall cohesion of the group. By fostering an environment where all voices were heard, Neon Frequencies was able to synthesize their differing ideas into a cohesive sound.

The Outcome

The resolution of these creative differences not only strengthened the band's dynamic but also resulted in the creation of some of their most beloved tracks. The album that emerged from this tumultuous period showcased a fusion of styles, blending Dabin's experimental tendencies with the band's rock roots. Critics praised the innovative sound, noting that it was a testament to the band's ability to navigate their differences and emerge stronger.

In conclusion, while creative differences can pose significant challenges, they also serve as a catalyst for growth and innovation. For Neon Frequencies, the journey through conflict and resolution was integral to their artistic development. By embracing their diverse perspectives and fostering a culture of open communication, they transformed potential discord into a powerful creative force, ultimately solidifying their place in the music industry.

The Battle with Addiction and Mental Health

The journey of a musician is often a double-edged sword, where the highs of creative expression can be shadowed by the lows of personal struggles. For Dabin and the members of Neon Frequencies, the pressures of fame and the relentless pursuit of success took a toll on their mental health, leading to battles with addiction that would challenge the very foundation of their artistry.

Understanding Addiction in the Music Industry

Addiction is a complex condition characterized by compulsive substance use despite harmful consequences. In the music industry, the allure of drugs and alcohol can be particularly potent, often glamorized as part of the rock 'n' roll lifestyle. According to the *American Psychiatric Association*, addiction alters the brain's natural balance of neurotransmitters, leading to a cycle of dependence that can be difficult to break.

The musicians' environment, filled with late-night parties and the pressure to perform, creates a perfect storm for substance abuse. The National Institute on Drug Abuse (NIDA) highlights that the prevalence of substance use disorders is significantly higher among musicians compared to the general population, with stress, anxiety, and depression being common precursors.

Dabin's Struggles

For Dabin, the pressures of touring and the demands of the music industry began to manifest in unhealthy coping mechanisms. Initially, the late-night celebrations after successful shows seemed harmless, but as the pressures mounted, what started as casual use spiraled into dependency. The exhilaration of performing was often followed by a crash, leading Dabin to seek solace in substances to numb the emotional turmoil.

In interviews, Dabin reflected on the isolation that often accompanies fame. "You're surrounded by people, yet you feel utterly alone," she stated. This paradox can lead to a reliance on drugs and alcohol as a means to escape the loneliness that fame brings.

The Impact on the Band

As Dabin grappled with her addiction, it began to affect the dynamics within Neon Frequencies. The bandmates noticed changes in her behavior—mood swings, decreased motivation, and a growing distance during rehearsals. The chemistry that once fueled their creative process was strained, leading to conflicts over artistic direction and personal priorities.

The *Journal of Substance Abuse Treatment* suggests that interpersonal relationships can significantly impact recovery. For Neon Frequencies, the bond between band members became both a source of support and a point of contention. While some members advocated for a more open dialogue about mental health, others were reluctant to confront the issue, fearing it might jeopardize the band's success.

Seeking Help

Recognizing the need for intervention, Dabin eventually sought help through rehabilitation programs. The process of recovery is often nonlinear, filled with relapses and breakthroughs. According to the *Substance Abuse and Mental Health Services Administration* (SAMHSA), effective treatment incorporates a range of therapies, including cognitive-behavioral therapy (CBT), which helps individuals understand the thoughts and feelings that contribute to their substance use.

Dabin's journey through rehab was not just about overcoming addiction but also about addressing the underlying mental health issues that fueled her dependency. Through therapy, she learned to confront her anxiety and depression, developing healthier coping strategies.

The Role of Support Systems

The support of her bandmates played a crucial role in Dabin's recovery. They attended family therapy sessions together, fostering an environment of understanding and empathy. This collective effort not only strengthened their bond but also revitalized their music, allowing them to channel their experiences into their songwriting.

The importance of a strong support system is emphasized in the *American Journal of Psychiatry*, which states that social support can significantly enhance recovery outcomes. For Neon Frequencies, this meant not only addressing individual struggles but also reinforcing their commitment to each other as a band.

Lessons Learned and Moving Forward

As Dabin emerged from her battles with addiction and mental health, she became an advocate for mental health awareness within the music community. She began to use her platform to speak openly about her experiences, encouraging others to seek help and fostering a culture of acceptance around mental health issues.

The impact of her journey is evident in the band's music, which evolved to reflect themes of resilience, vulnerability, and healing. Songs that once centered around the euphoria of fame now delve into the complexities of mental health, resonating deeply with fans who have faced similar struggles.

In conclusion, the battle with addiction and mental health is a poignant chapter in the story of Dabin and Neon Frequencies. It serves as a reminder that behind the glitz and glamour of the music industry lies a human experience filled with challenges. By addressing these issues head-on, Dabin not only reclaimed her life and artistry but also inspired a generation of musicians to prioritize their mental health, proving that vulnerability can be a powerful catalyst for change.

Unforgettable Concert Moments and Career Milestones

The journey of **Neon Frequencies** has been punctuated by a series of unforgettable concert moments and significant career milestones that not only defined their trajectory but also solidified their place in the hearts of fans around the world. Each performance, each milestone, serves as a testament to the band's resilience, creativity, and the indelible connection they have fostered with their audience.

The First Major Gig

One of the defining moments in the band's early career was their first major gig at the *Sunset Music Festival*. This festival, known for its eclectic lineup and vibrant atmosphere, provided the perfect platform for Neon Frequencies to showcase their unique sound. The anticipation was palpable, as the band had spent countless hours rehearsing and perfecting their setlist.

As they took the stage, the energy in the air was electric. The crowd, a mix of local music lovers and festival-goers, erupted into cheers. The opening notes of their hit single, "*Electric Dreams*", reverberated through the venue, and in that moment, the band felt an overwhelming sense of belonging. This performance not only marked a significant milestone in their career but also set the stage for their rise to fame.

The Breakthrough Performance

Fast forward to their performance at the *Global Music Awards*, where Neon Frequencies was nominated for *Best New Artist*. This was more than just an awards show; it was a pivotal moment that would catapult them into the mainstream. The band delivered a breathtaking performance that combined stunning visuals with their signature sound, leaving the audience in awe.

The culmination of this performance was when they received the award for *Best New Artist*. The moment was surreal, and as Dabin took the stage to accept the award, she delivered an emotional speech that resonated deeply with fans and fellow artists alike. This recognition not only validated their hard work but also opened doors for new opportunities, including collaborations with established artists and invitations to perform at prestigious venues worldwide.

The Stadium Tour

One of the most significant career milestones for Neon Frequencies was their first stadium tour. The *Neon Nights Tour* was a monumental undertaking that showcased their growth as artists and their ability to connect with fans on a grand scale. The tour included sold-out shows at iconic venues such as *Madison Square Garden* and the *O2 Arena*.

The logistics of a stadium tour presented numerous challenges, from stage design to sound engineering, but the band embraced these challenges with enthusiasm. Each concert was a celebration, with elaborate light shows, stunning visuals, and high-energy performances that left fans breathless. The tour not only solidified their status as rock stars but also demonstrated their commitment to delivering unforgettable experiences to their audience.

Iconic Collaborations

Throughout their career, Neon Frequencies has had the privilege of collaborating with some of the biggest names in the music industry. One such collaboration was with the legendary producer *Max Martin*. This partnership resulted in the creation of their chart-topping single, "Chasing the Stars", which became an anthem for a generation.

The creative process behind this collaboration was both exhilarating and challenging. Dabin and her bandmates worked tirelessly in the studio, pushing the boundaries of their sound while staying true to their roots. The result was a song that resonated with fans across the globe, further solidifying Neon Frequencies' place in music history.

Memorable Fan Interactions

Concerts are not just about the music; they are also about the connection between artists and fans. Neon Frequencies has always prioritized this connection, and memorable fan interactions have become a hallmark of their performances.

One particularly poignant moment occurred during a concert in *Tokyo*, where a fan presented Dabin with a handmade gift—a scrapbook filled with letters and memories from fans around the world. Dabin was visibly moved, and she took a moment to express her gratitude to the fan and the audience. This interaction highlighted the profound impact that music can have on people's lives and reinforced the bond between the band and their fans.

Awards and Recognition

The accolades and recognition that Neon Frequencies has received over the years serve as milestones that mark their evolution as artists. From winning multiple *Grammy Awards* to being featured in prestigious music publications, each award has been a validation of their hard work and dedication to their craft.

One of the most memorable nights was at the *Billboard Music Awards*, where they won the award for *Top Rock Artist*. The band took the stage to accept the award, and the moment was filled with emotion and gratitude. Dabin's speech, which highlighted the importance of pursuing one's passion and staying true to oneself, resonated with many aspiring musicians in the audience.

Legacy and Impact

As Neon Frequencies continues to evolve and grow, their unforgettable concert moments and career milestones will remain etched in the memories of fans and fellow artists alike. Each performance, each award, and each interaction with fans contributes to the legacy they are building—a legacy that inspires future generations of musicians to pursue their dreams and create music that resonates with the world.

In conclusion, the journey of Neon Frequencies is a testament to the power of music and the connections it fosters. Their unforgettable concert moments and significant career milestones serve as reminders of the passion, dedication, and creativity that define their artistry. As they continue to push boundaries and explore new horizons, fans eagerly await what the future holds for this remarkable band.

Awards, Accolades, and the Price of Success

The journey of Neon Frequencies has been marked by a series of monumental achievements that not only solidified their place in the music industry but also came with a unique set of challenges. The accolades received by the band are a testament to their hard work, creativity, and the connection they fostered with their fans. However, with success often comes a price, and navigating this complex landscape is a vital chapter in the story of Dabin and her bandmates.

Recognition and Awards

From the outset, Neon Frequencies was a force to be reckoned with. Their debut album, *Neon Dreams*, was met with critical acclaim, leading to several nominations and awards. The album won the prestigious **Best New Artist** at the *Global Music Awards*, which catapulted them into the limelight. This award was not just a trophy; it symbolized the hard work and dedication that the band poured into their music.

As their career progressed, they collected numerous accolades, including:

- **Grammy Awards:** Nominated for *Best Pop Duo/Group Performance* for their hit single "Electric Heart."

- **MTV Music Video Awards:** Winner of *Best Art Direction* for the visually stunning video of "Neon Nights."

- **Billboard Music Awards:** Recognition as *Top Rock Artist* and *Top Rock Album* for their sophomore release.

These accolades not only served to validate their artistic endeavors but also opened doors to new opportunities, including collaborations with high-profile artists and invitations to perform at renowned festivals worldwide.

The Burden of Success

However, the glitz and glamour of success brought with it an array of pressures that the band had to navigate. The expectations set by their newfound fame often felt like an insurmountable weight. The pressure to consistently produce chart-topping hits and maintain public interest led to intense scrutiny from the media and fans alike.

Creative Pressure One of the most significant challenges was the creative pressure that came with their success. The equation for success in the music industry can often be simplified to:

$$S = C + E + M$$

Where:

- S = Success
- C = Creativity (the originality and artistic expression)
- E = Engagement (the connection with fans)
- M = Marketability (the commercial appeal)

As Neon Frequencies continued to rise, the band felt the need to innovate constantly. This led to a cycle of self-doubt and anxiety, particularly for Dabin, who often felt responsible for the band's creative direction. The fear of not meeting expectations sometimes overshadowed the joy of making music.

Personal Struggles The personal lives of the band members also suffered due to their relentless pursuit of success. Late-night parties and the rockstar lifestyle often masked deeper issues. The equation for personal well-being in the face of fame can be expressed as:

$$W = H + R - S$$

Where:

- W = Well-being
- H = Happiness (personal fulfillment and joy)
- R = Relationships (support from family and friends)
- S = Stress (from fame and industry pressures)

As the stress of their career mounted, some members struggled with mental health issues, leading to conflicts within the band. The balance between personal happiness and professional obligations became increasingly precarious.

The Cost of Fame

The price of success was not only emotional but also financial. The band faced the harsh reality of the music industry, where the cost of touring, production, and promotion could quickly outweigh their earnings. This financial strain often led to discussions about the sustainability of their career.

Moreover, the constant travel and time away from home took a toll on personal relationships. Dabin's relationships with her family and friends became strained, as the demands of her career left little room for personal connections. The emotional cost of success manifested in feelings of isolation, as Dabin often found herself surrounded by people yet feeling profoundly alone.

Conclusion

In conclusion, while the accolades and awards that Neon Frequencies garnered were significant milestones, they came with a complex array of challenges. The band learned that success is not merely defined by trophies and recognition but also by the ability to navigate the pressures that accompany it. As they moved forward, they sought to embrace both their achievements and the lessons learned along the way, understanding that the journey is as important as the destination. The story of Neon Frequencies is a powerful reminder that with great success comes great responsibility, both to oneself and to the art they create.

Evolution and Growth

Evolution and Growth

Evolution and Growth

The evolution of an artist is often marked by significant transformations that reflect not only their artistic journey but also their personal growth. In the case of Dabin and Neon Frequencies, this evolution is a tapestry woven from various influences, experiences, and creative explorations. This chapter delves into the multi-faceted evolution of Dabin, exploring how her musical journey has shaped the sound and identity of Neon Frequencies, and how the band itself has adapted to the ever-changing landscape of the music industry.

The Musical Evolution of Dabin

Dabin's journey is characterized by a relentless pursuit of innovation and a desire to break genre boundaries. This section examines how her exploration of new sounds has not only influenced her solo work but also redefined the essence of Neon Frequencies.

Breaking Genres: Dabin's Exploration into New Sounds Dabin's artistic philosophy centers around the idea that music should be an ever-evolving expression of one's self. This belief has led her to experiment with a plethora of musical styles, from electronic and pop to rock and acoustic. The integration of diverse genres can be understood through the lens of genre theory, which posits that music is not confined to rigid categories but is instead a fluid spectrum of sound.

In her pursuit of innovation, Dabin often draws inspiration from her surroundings and the cultural zeitgeist. For example, her collaboration with electronic music producers has resulted in a fusion of traditional melodies with contemporary beats, creating a sound that resonates with a wide audience. This blending of genres is exemplified in her track "Electric Heart," where she combines synth-heavy beats with acoustic guitar riffs, showcasing her versatility and willingness to push creative boundaries.

Solo Ventures: Dabin's Side Projects and Collaborations Dabin's solo ventures have provided her with the freedom to explore her artistic identity outside the confines of the band. These projects often serve as a testing ground for new ideas and concepts that can later be incorporated into Neon Frequencies' music.

One notable example is her collaboration with indie artist Lila, where they co-wrote the song "Waves of Tomorrow." This track not only highlights Dabin's ability to adapt her style but also reflects her commitment to collaboration as a means of artistic growth. The success of this project reinforced her belief in the power of collaboration, leading to more experimental works that would eventually influence the band's sound.

Dabin's Influence on Neon Frequencies' Sound As Dabin evolved as an artist, so too did the sound of Neon Frequencies. Her growing confidence in her musical abilities allowed her to take on a more prominent role in the band's creative process. This shift is evident in their second album, where Dabin's songwriting and production skills are at the forefront.

The band's sound, once characterized by a more traditional rock aesthetic, began to incorporate electronic elements, resulting in a richer, more dynamic auditory experience. The equation below illustrates the relationship between Dabin's individual contributions and the overall sound of Neon Frequencies:

$$S = f(D, E, C) \qquad (45)$$

where S represents the overall sound of Neon Frequencies, D denotes Dabin's individual contributions, E represents the contributions of other band members, and C signifies the collaborative efforts in songwriting and production. This equation emphasizes the interdependence of individual and collective creativity within the band.

The Second Album: Reinventing the Neon Frequencies Sound

The release of Neon Frequencies' second album marked a pivotal moment in their career. This section explores the creative vision behind the album, the struggles faced during the recording process, and the reception from both fans and critics.

EVOLUTION AND GROWTH

Dabin's Creative Vision: A New Direction With the second album, Dabin sought to redefine the band's identity. Her vision encompassed a more experimental approach, incorporating elements of electronic music, world music, and even classical influences. This desire for innovation is rooted in the concept of artistic identity, which suggests that an artist's work is a reflection of their personal experiences and aspirations.

Dabin's vision was not without its challenges. The band faced internal conflicts regarding the direction of their sound, leading to heated discussions during the songwriting process. However, these conflicts ultimately resulted in a more cohesive and authentic sound, as each member contributed their unique perspectives.

The Recording Process: Struggles and Breakthroughs The recording process for the second album was fraught with difficulties, including technical issues and creative disagreements. However, these struggles served as catalysts for growth. The band learned to navigate their differences, emerging stronger and more unified.

An example of this breakthrough can be seen in the track "Chasing Shadows," where the initial version was deemed unsatisfactory by the band. After several revisions and a collaborative effort to reimagine the song, it transformed into one of their most beloved tracks. This experience underscored the importance of resilience and adaptability in the creative process.

Critical and Commercial Reception of the Second Album Upon its release, the second album received critical acclaim, with many praising its innovative sound and lyrical depth. The fusion of genres resonated with fans and critics alike, leading to increased visibility for Neon Frequencies. The success of the album can be attributed to Dabin's willingness to take risks and explore new artistic territories.

In conclusion, the evolution of Dabin and Neon Frequencies is a testament to the power of creativity, collaboration, and resilience. As they continue to grow and adapt to the ever-changing music landscape, their journey serves as an inspiration for aspiring musicians and fans alike. The next chapter will delve deeper into the personal and professional growth of Dabin and the band, exploring how their experiences have shaped their identity and legacy in the music industry.

The Musical Evolution of Dabin

Breaking Genres: Dabin's Exploration into New Sounds

Dabin's journey into the realm of musical innovation is a testament to the dynamic nature of contemporary music. As she ventured beyond the traditional boundaries of genres, she embraced a multitude of influences, resulting in a sound that is uniquely her own. This exploration is not merely a quest for novelty; it is a deep-rooted desire to express the complexities of human emotion and experience through sound.

Theoretical Framework

The exploration of new sounds can be understood through the lens of genre theory, which posits that music genres are not fixed categories but rather fluid constructs that evolve over time. According to [?], genres serve as a means for listeners to make sense of the vast array of musical expressions available to them. In this context, Dabin's work can be seen as a challenge to the conventional genre classifications, pushing the boundaries of what is considered acceptable within the music industry.

The Problem of Genre Classification

One of the significant challenges in Dabin's exploration is the problem of genre classification. As she incorporates elements from electronic, rock, pop, and even classical music, critics and fans alike often struggle to categorize her work. This ambiguity can lead to misunderstandings and misrepresentations of her artistic vision. For instance, her single "Echoes of Tomorrow" features a blend of heavy guitar riffs and ethereal synths, creating a soundscape that defies easy classification.

$$\text{Genre Complexity} = f(\text{Electronic} + \text{Rock} + \text{Pop} + \text{Classical}) \quad (46)$$

This equation illustrates the complexity of Dabin's genre fusion, where each musical style contributes to a richer and more diverse auditory experience.

Examples of Genre-Bending Tracks

Dabin's discography is replete with examples of her genre-bending capabilities. The track "Neon Dreams" exemplifies her ability to merge electronic beats with emotive lyrics, drawing inspiration from both pop and indie genres. The song opens with a pulsating synth line, gradually introducing layers of acoustic instrumentation, creating a contrast that captivates listeners.

Similarly, in "Vortex," Dabin experiments with time signatures and rhythmic patterns traditionally found in progressive rock. By incorporating polyrhythms and syncopation, she challenges the listener's expectations, inviting them to engage with the music on a deeper level. This track highlights her willingness to take risks, as she deftly navigates the complexities of rhythm and melody.

Collaborative Ventures

Collaboration has also played a pivotal role in Dabin's exploration of new sounds. By working with artists from diverse musical backgrounds, she has expanded her sonic palette. A notable example is her collaboration with electronic producer *Kaskade* on the track "Lost in the Lights." This partnership not only showcases Dabin's versatility but also highlights the importance of cross-genre collaborations in contemporary music.

The fusion of Kaskade's house music influences with Dabin's melodic sensibilities results in a track that resonates with a broad audience, further illustrating the potential for genre-blending to create innovative musical experiences.

The Impact of Technology

Technological advancements have also played a crucial role in Dabin's exploration of new sounds. The advent of digital audio workstations (DAWs) has democratized music production, allowing artists to experiment with sounds that were previously inaccessible. Dabin's use of software like *Ableton Live* enables her to manipulate sound in real-time, creating intricate layers and textures that challenge traditional notions of composition.

This technological prowess is evident in her live performances, where she seamlessly integrates live instrumentation with pre-recorded elements, crafting an immersive experience for her audience. The interplay between technology and artistry exemplifies the contemporary musician's toolkit, empowering artists like Dabin to break free from genre constraints.

Conclusion

In conclusion, Dabin's exploration into new sounds represents a significant departure from conventional genre boundaries. By embracing a multitude of influences and utilizing modern technology, she has forged a path that is uniquely her own. The complexities of genre classification may pose challenges, but they also serve as a testament to the richness of her artistry. As she continues to evolve, Dabin remains a beacon of innovation in the ever-changing landscape of music.

Solo Ventures: Dabin's Side Projects and Collaborations

As the vibrant soundscapes of Neon Frequencies began to resonate across the globe, Dabin found herself at a creative crossroads. The allure of solo ventures beckoned, promising a canvas where she could explore her artistic identity beyond the confines of the band. These side projects and collaborations would not only showcase her versatility but also enrich the sonic palette of her primary band, Neon Frequencies.

Exploring New Genres

Dabin's solo endeavors allowed her to delve into genres that were often sidelined within the band's collective sound. For instance, her collaboration with electronic producer *Xavier Blaze* on the track *"Elysium"* showcased a blend of synthwave and ambient music. The track's ethereal melodies and pulsating bass lines created a hypnotic atmosphere, illustrating Dabin's ability to transcend traditional genre boundaries. This collaboration was not just a musical experiment; it was a testament to her willingness to embrace change and innovation.

Collaborative Synergy

One of the most significant aspects of Dabin's solo work was her collaboration with various artists. In 2021, she teamed up with singer-songwriter *Ella Voss* on the emotionally charged ballad *"Fragments."* The song's poignant lyrics and haunting harmonies resonated with listeners, earning critical acclaim. Dabin's ability to harmonize and create intricate vocal layers with Voss highlighted her prowess as a vocalist and songwriter. The synergy between the two artists created a powerful emotional connection, demonstrating how collaboration can elevate artistic expression.

Thematic Exploration

Dabin's solo projects often explored themes that were personal and introspective. In her EP *"Reflections,"* released in 2022, she delved into topics such as identity, love, and loss. The lead single, *"Mirror,"* was a raw and vulnerable exploration of self-acceptance. The accompanying music video, featuring stunning visuals of Dabin in various reflective settings, further amplified the song's message. This project marked a significant evolution in her songwriting, as she began to draw from her own life experiences to craft relatable narratives.

Live Performances and Solo Tours

Dabin's solo ventures also translated into live performances, where she showcased her new material. The *"Dabin Unplugged"* tour, which featured intimate acoustic sets, allowed her to connect with fans on a deeper level. The stripped-down arrangements of her songs highlighted her vocal strengths and songwriting abilities. During these performances, Dabin often included stories behind her songs, creating a narrative thread that engaged the audience and fostered a sense of community.

Cross-Genre Collaborations

In a bold move, Dabin ventured into the realm of hip-hop by collaborating with rapper *KJ Flow* on the track *"Rhythm of the Night."* The fusion of her melodic sensibilities with KJ's dynamic flow created a fresh sound that captivated listeners. This collaboration not only broadened her artistic horizons but also attracted a new audience to her music. The success of *"Rhythm of the Night"* exemplified the power of cross-genre collaborations, proving that music knows no boundaries.

Production and Songwriting Credits

Beyond performing, Dabin began to take on production and songwriting roles for other artists. Her work with up-and-coming singer *Mia Chen* on the track *"Chasing Shadows"* showcased her skills as a producer. Dabin's keen ear for arrangement and sound design played a crucial role in shaping the song's final form. This transition into a behind-the-scenes role allowed her to influence the music industry in a new way, as she nurtured emerging talents and contributed to their artistic journeys.

Impact on Neon Frequencies

Dabin's solo ventures had a profound impact on Neon Frequencies as well. The experiences and insights gained from her side projects enriched her contributions to the band. Her exploration of different genres and collaboration styles brought fresh ideas to the table, allowing the band to evolve its sound. As Dabin experimented with various musical elements, she introduced new textures and layers that would later be incorporated into Neon Frequencies' subsequent albums.

Legacy of Collaboration

Ultimately, Dabin's solo ventures and collaborations serve as a testament to her artistic growth and versatility. They highlight the importance of collaboration in the music industry, showcasing how artists can inspire and elevate one another. As she continues to navigate her solo career alongside Neon Frequencies, Dabin remains a beacon of creativity, proving that true artistry knows no bounds. Her journey exemplifies the notion that in music, collaboration is not just a means to an end; it is a vital part of the artistic process that fosters innovation and connection.

In conclusion, Dabin's solo ventures and collaborations illustrate her multifaceted talent and her commitment to pushing the boundaries of her artistry. Each project, each collaboration, adds a new layer to her musical identity, ensuring that her contributions to both her solo work and Neon Frequencies will be remembered as a significant chapter in the evolution of contemporary music.

Dabin's Influence on Neon Frequencies' Sound

Dabin's impact on the sound of Neon Frequencies is both profound and multifaceted, weaving together elements of innovation, emotional depth, and genre-blending that have become hallmarks of the band's identity. From the very inception of the group, Dabin's unique musical perspective shaped their sonic landscape, pushing boundaries and inviting a diverse array of influences into their work.

At the core of Dabin's influence is her ability to seamlessly integrate various musical styles. Drawing from her rich musical family background, Dabin was exposed to a plethora of genres during her formative years. This eclectic foundation allowed her to experiment with different sounds, leading to the creation of a genre-defying style that became synonymous with Neon Frequencies. The mathematical representation of this integration can be expressed through a function $f(x)$ that combines multiple variables representing different genres:

$$f(x) = a_1 \cdot \text{Genre}_1 + a_2 \cdot \text{Genre}_2 + a_3 \cdot \text{Genre}_3 + \ldots + a_n \cdot \text{Genre}_n$$

where a_i represents the influence coefficient of each genre on the overall sound of the band. This function illustrates how Dabin's diverse influences coalesce to form a cohesive yet dynamic sound.

Dabin's contributions to songwriting also played a pivotal role in shaping the band's identity. Her lyrical prowess brought depth and relatability to the band's music, allowing fans to connect on a personal level. The emotional resonance of her lyrics can be analyzed through the lens of music theory, particularly the concept of tension and release. Dabin often employed harmonic progressions that create a sense of longing or anticipation, resolved through poignant melodies. For example, the use of the ii-V-I progression is a staple in her songwriting, providing a familiar yet satisfying resolution that resonates with listeners:

$$\text{Tension} \to \text{ii} \to \text{V} \to \text{Release} \to \text{I}$$

This technique not only enhances the emotional impact of the music but also showcases Dabin's deep understanding of musical structure.

Moreover, Dabin's innovative approach to instrumentation has left a lasting mark on Neon Frequencies' sound. By incorporating non-traditional instruments and electronic elements, she has expanded the band's sonic palette. The use of synthesizers, for instance, adds layers of texture that elevate the overall production quality. The equation governing the relationship between instrumentation and sound quality can be expressed as:

$$SQ = \sum_{i=1}^{n}(I_i \cdot E_i)$$

where SQ represents sound quality, I_i denotes the individual instruments used, and E_i represents the effects applied to those instruments. Dabin's keen sense of how to manipulate these variables has resulted in a rich auditory experience that captivates audiences.

Another significant aspect of Dabin's influence is her collaborative spirit. Her ability to inspire and elevate her bandmates has fostered a creative environment where innovation thrives. The collaborative process can be modeled as a system of equations that reflects the interactions between band members:

$$C = \sum_{j=1}^{m}(D_j + B_j)$$

where C is the overall creativity of the band, D_j represents Dabin's contributions, and B_j denotes the contributions of each bandmate. This synergy has led to the creation of songs that are not only technically proficient but also deeply resonant.

In conclusion, Dabin's influence on Neon Frequencies' sound is a complex interplay of various musical elements, emotional depth, and collaborative creativity. Her ability to blend genres, craft poignant lyrics, innovate with instrumentation, and inspire her bandmates has culminated in a unique sound that continues to evolve. As Neon Frequencies forges ahead, Dabin's indelible mark will undoubtedly resonate through their music, ensuring that their legacy remains as vibrant as the neon lights that inspire their name.

The Second Album: Reinventing the Neon Frequencies Sound

Dabin's Creative Vision: A New Direction

Dabin's journey into the realm of music has always been characterized by an insatiable desire to innovate and explore the uncharted territories of sound. As Neon Frequencies began to solidify its presence in the music industry, Dabin recognized that the band's evolution was not merely a natural progression but a conscious effort to redefine their artistic identity. This section delves into Dabin's creative vision for the band's second album, which aimed to take their sound in a bold new direction.

The Conceptual Framework

At the heart of Dabin's new direction lay a conceptual framework that sought to challenge the conventional boundaries of genre. The primary goal was to transcend the limitations imposed by traditional music classifications, allowing for a fluid amalgamation of styles. Dabin believed that music should not be confined to rigid categories; instead, it should reflect the complexity of human emotions and experiences. This idea is encapsulated in the following equation, which represents the fusion of genres as a dynamic interplay:

$$S = \sum_{i=1}^{n} G_i \cdot W_i \qquad (47)$$

Where: - S is the resultant sound. - G_i represents each genre incorporated into the music. - W_i is the weight or influence of each genre on the final composition.

This equation illustrates Dabin's approach to songwriting, where multiple genres are interwoven to create a rich tapestry of sound, resonating with a diverse audience.

Thematic Exploration

Dabin's creative vision was also marked by a deeper thematic exploration. The lyrics of the second album were intended to reflect the complexities of modern life, addressing themes such as identity, love, loss, and the search for meaning in an increasingly chaotic world. Dabin drew inspiration from personal experiences, as well as societal issues, aiming to create a narrative that would resonate with listeners on a profound level.

For example, the track *"Echoes of Tomorrow"* delves into the struggle of self-discovery amidst societal expectations. The chorus encapsulates the essence of this theme:

> "Echoes of tomorrow, whispering my name, In a world of shadows, I'm searching for the flame."

Such lyrics not only showcase Dabin's introspective nature but also invite listeners to engage with their own journeys.

Collaborative Synergy

Recognizing the importance of collaboration, Dabin sought to bring in a diverse array of artists and producers to contribute to the album. This collaborative synergy was essential in achieving the desired sound, as different perspectives and influences enriched the creative process. The result was a dynamic interplay of ideas, leading to innovative compositions that pushed the boundaries of what Neon Frequencies could achieve.

One notable collaboration was with electronic music producer *Luna Beats*, whose expertise in synthesizers and sound design added a fresh dimension to the album. Together, they experimented with various soundscapes, resulting in tracks like *"Fractured Reality"*, which seamlessly blended organic instrumentation with electronic elements.

Challenges and Triumphs

However, this ambitious creative vision was not without its challenges. The process of redefining the band's sound often led to tensions within the group, as differing opinions on musical direction emerged. Dabin, as the creative force, had to navigate these conflicts while maintaining a cohesive vision.

One significant challenge was the balancing act between artistic integrity and commercial viability. Dabin was acutely aware that pushing boundaries could alienate some of their existing fanbase. This dilemma is reflected in the equation:

$$C = f(A, V) \tag{48}$$

Where: - C represents commercial success. - A denotes artistic expression. - V signifies the value perceived by the audience.

Dabin's approach involved finding a sweet spot where artistic expression could flourish without sacrificing the band's connection with its audience. This required a delicate negotiation of sounds and themes, ultimately leading to a more authentic representation of their artistic vision.

Conclusion: A New Era for Neon Frequencies

In conclusion, Dabin's creative vision for the second album of Neon Frequencies marked a pivotal moment in the band's evolution. By embracing a genre-defying approach, exploring profound themes, fostering collaborative synergy, and navigating the challenges of artistic growth, Dabin not only redefined the band's sound but also set the stage for a new era in their musical journey. This album would not only serve as a testament to their growth but also as an invitation for listeners to embark on a transformative experience alongside them.

As Neon Frequencies prepared to unveil their new direction, anticipation buzzed in the air. Dabin's vision was clear: to create music that resonated deeply, challenged norms, and ultimately transcended the boundaries of sound. This bold leap into the unknown would define not only the band's future but also the landscape of contemporary music.

The Recording Process: Struggles and Breakthroughs

The recording process for Neon Frequencies' second album was a journey marked by both struggles and breakthroughs, a testament to the band's resilience and creativity. This phase was not merely about capturing sound; it was a transformative experience that pushed the boundaries of their musical identity and tested their collaboration.

Navigating Creative Differences

As the band members delved into the recording studio, they quickly realized that the creative synergy that had initially brought them together was now facing challenges. Each member had evolved musically, and their individual influences began to clash. Dabin, in particular, was eager to explore new sounds and genres, inspired by emerging trends in the music industry. This led to moments of tension as some bandmates were hesitant to stray too far from their established sound.

To navigate these creative differences, the band implemented a structured approach to collaboration. They adopted a method known as *collaborative songwriting*, which involved brainstorming sessions where every member could voice their ideas without judgment. This process was guided by the principle that *diversity in creativity leads to innovation*. For example, during one session, Dabin suggested incorporating electronic elements into a traditionally acoustic song. Initially met with skepticism, this idea eventually blossomed into a breakthrough track that became a fan favorite.

Technical Challenges and Solutions

Recording in a professional studio came with its own set of technical challenges. The band faced issues with sound quality, mixing, and mastering. One significant problem arose during the recording of their lead single. The initial mix lacked clarity, causing the vocals to be overshadowed by the instrumental backdrop. Recognizing the need for improvement, the band brought in an experienced sound engineer who introduced advanced mixing techniques.

The engineer explained the importance of *frequency separation* in mixing, which involves ensuring that different instruments occupy distinct frequency ranges. This is mathematically represented as:

$$f_{total} = f_{instruments} + f_{vocals} + f_{effects}$$

Where f_{total} is the total frequency spectrum utilized in the mix. By applying this principle, they were able to achieve a more balanced sound, allowing each element to shine through.

Emotional Breakthroughs in the Studio

Amidst the technical and creative struggles, the recording process also became a space for emotional breakthroughs. The band members found themselves confronting personal issues that influenced their music. Dabin, for example, drew from her experiences of heartbreak and loss, channeling these emotions into her songwriting. This vulnerability resonated with her bandmates, leading to a deeper connection and understanding of each other's artistic visions.

One poignant moment occurred during the recording of a ballad, where Dabin's raw emotion during a vocal take brought the entire studio to silence. The power of her delivery transformed the song, turning it into a cathartic experience for both the band and the listeners. This incident underscored the theory that *authenticity in music fosters a genuine connection with the audience.*

Innovative Techniques and Experimentation

To further enhance their sound, the band embraced innovative recording techniques. They experimented with unconventional instruments and sounds, such as layering field recordings from their travels. This approach was inspired by the *found sound* movement, which emphasizes incorporating everyday noises into musical compositions.

For instance, the band recorded ambient sounds from a bustling city street, which were later woven into a track, creating a rich tapestry of audio that reflected their journey. This technique not only added depth to their music but also aligned with their goal of capturing the essence of their experiences.

Finalizing the Album: A Collective Effort

As the recording sessions progressed, the band learned to lean on each other's strengths. They established a routine that included regular feedback sessions, where they would listen to rough mixes and provide constructive criticism. This collaborative spirit was encapsulated in their motto: *"Together, we rise."*

The culmination of their efforts resulted in a cohesive album that showcased their growth as musicians. The struggles they faced during the recording process ultimately became a source of strength, leading to breakthroughs that defined their sound. The album was not just a collection of songs; it was a narrative of their journey, filled with the highs and lows of the creative process.

In conclusion, the recording process for Neon Frequencies was a complex interplay of struggles and breakthroughs. By embracing their differences, overcoming technical challenges, and fostering emotional connections, the band emerged stronger and more united. The lessons learned during this phase would resonate throughout their careers, shaping their future endeavors and solidifying their place in the music industry.

Critical and Commercial Reception of the Second Album

The release of Neon Frequencies' second album marked a pivotal moment in the band's trajectory, both critically and commercially. Following the success of their debut, expectations were sky-high, and the pressure to deliver a sophomore effort that could live up to its predecessor was palpable. This section delves into the reception of the album, exploring how it was received by critics and fans alike, as well as its impact on the band's career.

Critical Acclaim

Upon its release, the second album received a wave of critical acclaim from music journalists and industry experts. Many praised the band's evolution in sound, noting a significant maturation in their songwriting and production quality. Renowned music critic, Jane Doe, remarked in *Rolling Stone* that "Neon Frequencies has not only expanded their sonic palette but has also deepened their lyrical content, making this album a compelling listen from start to finish."

The album was lauded for its innovative blending of genres, incorporating elements of electronic, rock, and pop. Critics highlighted standout tracks such as "Electric Dreams" and "Echoes of Tomorrow," which showcased the band's ability to push boundaries while maintaining their signature sound. The incorporation of live instrumentation alongside electronic elements was noted as a bold move that resonated well with audiences.

Commercial Success

Commercially, the second album achieved remarkable success. It debuted at number one on the *Billboard 200* chart, a feat that solidified Neon Frequencies' status as a household name in the music industry. The lead single, "Electric Dreams," quickly climbed the charts, reaching the top ten in multiple countries and earning platinum certification within months of its release.

The album's commercial performance can be quantitatively analyzed using the following equation, which represents the correlation between album sales (S), radio play (R), and streaming numbers (T):

$$S = k(R + T)$$

where k is a constant that represents the market's response to promotional efforts and the band's existing fanbase. In this case, the band's robust promotional campaign and their established fan loyalty contributed significantly to the album's sales figures.

The album's success was further bolstered by a series of high-profile performances, including appearances at major music festivals and a national tour that sold out in record time. The combination of strong radio play and viral social media engagement created a perfect storm for commercial success.

Fan Reception and Impact

Fans responded enthusiastically to the new material, with many expressing their appreciation for the band's growth and willingness to experiment. Online platforms such as Twitter and Instagram were flooded with positive feedback, with fans sharing their favorite tracks and personal stories related to the music. The hashtag #NeonFrequencies2 trended on multiple occasions, reflecting the album's cultural impact.

However, not all feedback was positive. Some long-time fans expressed concerns that the band had strayed too far from their original sound. This dichotomy in reception highlights an important aspect of artistic evolution: the balance between innovation and staying true to one's roots. While many embraced the new direction, a vocal minority felt nostalgic for the band's earlier style.

Awards and Recognition

The critical and commercial success of the second album translated into numerous award nominations and wins. It was nominated for several prestigious awards, including the *Grammy Awards* for Best Pop Vocal Album and Best Engineered Album, Non-Classical. The accolades served to further cement Neon Frequencies' place in the music industry and showcased their ability to compete with established artists.

In conclusion, the critical and commercial reception of Neon Frequencies' second album was overwhelmingly positive. The band not only met but exceeded the expectations set by their debut, paving the way for future projects and solidifying their legacy in the music world. The album's success was a testament to their hard work, creativity, and the deep connection they had forged with their audience. As they moved forward, the lessons learned from this experience would undoubtedly shape their future endeavors and artistic direction.

Personal and Professional Growth

Dabin's Solo Path: Solo Albums and Artistic Expression

Dabin's journey into solo artistry marks a significant evolution in her musical career, showcasing her ability to transcend the boundaries of her band, Neon Frequencies. This chapter delves into Dabin's solo albums and the artistic expression that flourished during this transformative period.

The Emergence of a Solo Artist

As the vibrant melodies of Neon Frequencies echoed across stages worldwide, Dabin felt an undeniable urge to explore her individuality. The decision to embark on a solo career was not merely a departure from her band; it was an opportunity to delve deeper into her creative psyche. The initial sparks of inspiration came from a desire to experiment with different genres and sounds that were not always aligned with the band's collective vision.

First Solo Album: *Echoes of the Heart*

Dabin's debut solo album, *Echoes of the Heart*, was released to critical acclaim. The album's production was a labor of love, characterized by a blend of electronic beats, acoustic elements, and introspective lyrics. Thematically, the album explored personal experiences, relationships, and the complexities of self-identity. Dabin described this work as a "musical diary," where each track represented a chapter of her life.

The lead single, "Whispers in the Wind," became an anthem for many, resonating with listeners due to its haunting melody and relatable lyrics. The song's success can be attributed to its emotional depth, which was a departure from the more upbeat tracks typically associated with Neon Frequencies. The equation that encapsulates the album's success can be expressed as:

$$S = E + C + A$$

where S is the success of the single, E is the emotional resonance with the audience, C is the creative innovation in sound, and A is the overall artistic expression evident in the lyrics and composition.

Artistic Expression and Growth

The journey of creating *Echoes of the Heart* allowed Dabin to cultivate her artistic expression. She began to embrace her vulnerabilities, channeling her emotions into her music. The process of songwriting became a therapeutic outlet, enabling her to confront her fears and aspirations. This period of introspection and growth led to the development of a unique sound that combined various influences, from indie pop to ambient electronic.

Dabin's ability to articulate her experiences through music is reminiscent of the theories posited by psychologist Mihaly Csikszentmihalyi regarding "flow" in creative processes. Csikszentmihalyi suggests that artists experience a state of flow when they are fully immersed in their work, leading to heightened creativity and satisfaction. Dabin's creative process reflected this theory, as she often found herself lost in the music, resulting in authentic and compelling compositions.

Second Solo Album: *Shattered Reflections*

Building on the success of her debut, Dabin released her sophomore album, *Shattered Reflections*. This album marked a pivotal point in her career, as it showcased her growth as both a musician and a storyteller. Thematically, *Shattered Reflections* dealt with the complexities of fame, personal struggles, and the quest for authenticity in a world that often demands conformity.

The single "Fragments" exemplified this evolution, combining intricate soundscapes with profound lyrics that explored the dichotomy of public perception versus personal reality. The song's structure employed a mix of complex time signatures and polyrhythms, pushing the boundaries of conventional pop music. This experimentation reflects the mathematical principles of rhythm and harmony, where the interplay of different elements creates a cohesive yet intricate musical experience.

Collaborations and Artistic Synergy

Dabin's solo path also opened doors for collaborations with other artists, further enriching her musical palette. Collaborating with diverse musicians allowed her to fuse different styles and genres, creating a melting pot of sounds. For instance, her collaboration with renowned producer Alex Chen on the track "Elysium" introduced elements of orchestral music, elevating the emotional impact of the song.

The synergy created through these collaborations can be understood through the lens of social constructivism, which posits that knowledge and meaning are constructed through social interactions. Dabin's collaborative efforts not only enhanced her artistic expression but also fostered a sense of community within the music industry, emphasizing the importance of shared creativity.

Impact on Neon Frequencies

Dabin's solo ventures had a profound impact on Neon Frequencies as well. Her exploration of new sounds and styles influenced the band's direction, leading to a more eclectic approach in their subsequent albums. The infusion of Dabin's solo experiences enriched the band's collective creativity, demonstrating the interconnectedness of individual artistry and group dynamics.

In conclusion, Dabin's solo path, marked by her albums *Echoes of the Heart* and *Shattered Reflections*, exemplifies her artistic evolution and dedication to self-expression. Through her music, she has not only carved out a distinct identity as a solo artist but also contributed to the broader narrative of Neon Frequencies. As she continues to explore new horizons in her musical journey, Dabin remains a beacon of inspiration for aspiring artists seeking to embrace their authenticity in a world of conformity.

The Band's Evolution: New Bandmates and Musical Directions

As Neon Frequencies progressed through their musical journey, the dynamics within the band began to evolve, leading to the introduction of new bandmates and a shift in musical direction. This evolution was not merely a matter of personnel changes; it represented a profound transformation in the band's artistic identity and sound.

New Bandmates: A Fresh Perspective

The introduction of new members brought fresh influences and perspectives to the band. Each new bandmate contributed unique skills and styles, enriching the collective sound of Neon Frequencies. For instance, the addition of a new guitarist, known for his expertise in jazz and blues, opened up avenues for intricate solos and complex chord progressions that had previously been unexplored in the band's music. This shift can be understood through the lens of collaborative creativity, where diverse backgrounds enhance the creative output.

$$C = \frac{1}{n} \sum_{i=1}^{n} x_i \qquad (49)$$

In this equation, C represents the collaborative creativity of the band, n is the number of bandmates, and x_i represents the unique contributions of each member. As new members joined, the value of n increased, allowing for a greater variety of inputs and ideas, which in turn elevated the overall creativity of the group.

Musical Directions: Experimentation and Growth

With the inclusion of new bandmates, Neon Frequencies began to experiment with different genres and styles. This experimentation was not without its challenges, as the band had to navigate the complexities of blending various influences. For example, the integration of electronic elements into their music marked a significant departure from their earlier, more traditional rock sound. This shift can be analyzed through the concept of genre hybridity, which refers to the blending of distinct musical styles to create something new and innovative.

The following equation illustrates the concept of genre hybridity in music:

$$H = \sum_{j=1}^{m} p_j \cdot g_j \qquad (50)$$

Where H represents the level of hybridity, m is the number of genres being blended, p_j is the proportion of each genre, and g_j is the unique characteristics of each genre. As Neon Frequencies incorporated electronic, pop, and rock elements, their music evolved into a distinct sound that resonated with a broader audience.

Challenges of Evolution

The evolution of the band was not without its challenges. As new members joined, there were inevitable growing pains. Differences in musical vision and creative disagreements sometimes led to tension within the group. For instance, the introduction of a new drummer who favored a more experimental and progressive style clashed with the existing members who were more rooted in traditional rock rhythms.

To address these conflicts, the band implemented a structured approach to collaboration, which involved regular brainstorming sessions and open discussions about musical direction. This approach allowed for the resolution of conflicts and fostered an environment of mutual respect and understanding. The equation below represents the balance of creative input and conflict resolution:

$$R = \frac{C_i}{C_i + D} \qquad (51)$$

In this equation, R represents the resolution of creative conflicts, C_i is the total creative input from all band members, and D is the degree of disagreement present. A higher value of R indicates a more harmonious creative process, allowing the band to evolve while maintaining a cohesive sound.

Examples of Musical Evolution

One notable example of this evolution is found in their second album, where the band ventured into uncharted territory by incorporating orchestral arrangements alongside their signature sound. This bold move not only showcased their versatility but also attracted a wider audience, demonstrating the power of evolution in music. The incorporation of strings and brass added depth and emotion to their tracks, illustrating the successful blending of different musical elements.

Moreover, the band's decision to collaborate with diverse artists from various genres further exemplified their evolution. By working with a hip-hop artist on one track, they were able to infuse rhythmic complexity and lyrical depth into their music, showcasing their willingness to embrace new influences and directions.

Conclusion

In conclusion, the evolution of Neon Frequencies through the introduction of new bandmates and musical directions has been a transformative journey. By embracing diversity in their lineup and experimenting with various genres, they have not only enriched their sound but also solidified their place in the music industry. The challenges faced along the way served as valuable lessons, ultimately leading to a stronger, more cohesive band. As they continue to evolve, the future of Neon Frequencies remains bright, promising even more innovative and groundbreaking music.

Keeping it Together: Balancing Personal Life and Stardom

The life of a musician is often romanticized, filled with glamour, adoration, and the thrill of performing in front of thousands. However, the reality of balancing personal life and stardom can be a tumultuous journey fraught with challenges. For Dabin and the members of Neon Frequencies, the quest for equilibrium between their soaring careers and personal lives often felt like walking a tightrope, where one misstep could lead to a fall into chaos.

The Duality of Fame

Fame brings with it a duality that can be both exhilarating and exhausting. On one hand, there are the accolades, the sold-out shows, and the endless opportunities for creative expression. On the other hand, the constant scrutiny from the public eye, the pressure to maintain a certain image, and the relentless demands of the music industry can take a toll on personal relationships.

Dabin, in particular, found herself navigating this complex landscape. As her star rose, she faced the challenge of maintaining relationships with family and friends who often felt the strain of her busy schedule. The theory of *social capital* suggests that the value of social networks can diminish if not nurtured. Dabin realized that while her professional life was thriving, her personal connections were at risk of stagnation.

Time Management: The Key to Balance

To manage the competing demands of her career and personal life, Dabin adopted rigorous time management strategies. By employing techniques such as the *Eisenhower Matrix*, she prioritized tasks based on urgency and importance. This approach allowed her to allocate time effectively, ensuring that both her professional obligations and personal commitments received attention.

Important and Urgent → Do FirstImportant but Not Urgent → ScheduleNot Important b
(52)

Dabin's ability to categorize her responsibilities helped her carve out precious moments for family gatherings, date nights, and self-care, which were essential for her mental well-being.

The Strain of Relationships

Despite her best efforts, the strain of fame inevitably impacted Dabin's relationships. The music industry often demands long hours, extensive travel, and a level of commitment that can overshadow personal connections. Dabin experienced moments of isolation, particularly during long tours when she was physically away from loved ones. The phenomenon of *relationship fatigue* became evident, as the emotional energy required to maintain connections waned under the pressures of her career.

For instance, during a particularly grueling tour, Dabin missed several family milestones, including her younger sister's graduation. The guilt and sadness that followed were palpable. This experience underscored the importance of *communication* in relationships. Dabin learned that open dialogue about her commitments and challenges was crucial in maintaining understanding and support from her loved ones.

Self-Care and Mental Health

Recognizing the toll that fame could take on her mental health, Dabin made self-care a priority. Engaging in activities such as yoga, meditation, and regular therapy sessions became integral to her routine. The theory of *self-care* posits that nurturing oneself is essential for sustaining the energy and resilience needed to navigate life's challenges.

Incorporating mindfulness practices not only helped Dabin manage stress but also enhanced her creativity. She often found that her best songwriting emerged from moments of introspection and self-reflection. By prioritizing her mental health, Dabin was able to return to her music with renewed vigor and passion.

Support Systems: The Band as Family

Throughout her journey, Dabin found solace in the support of her bandmates. The camaraderie within Neon Frequencies provided a unique buffer against the pressures of fame. They understood the challenges of balancing personal lives with their careers, having faced similar struggles themselves. This shared experience fostered a sense of belonging and mutual support that was invaluable.

The concept of *emotional labor* became evident as the band navigated their own challenges together. They often engaged in candid discussions about their feelings, fears, and aspirations, which helped them maintain a healthy dynamic. This open line of communication not only strengthened their bond but also allowed them to collaborate more effectively, resulting in a richer musical output.

Conclusion: The Ongoing Journey

The journey of balancing personal life and stardom is ongoing and ever-evolving. Dabin's experiences illustrate that while fame can bring extraordinary opportunities, it also demands a level of self-awareness and resilience. By prioritizing relationships, practicing self-care, and fostering a supportive environment, Dabin and her bandmates have been able to navigate the complexities of their lives in the spotlight.

Ultimately, the lessons learned from this journey extend beyond the music industry. They serve as a reminder that in the pursuit of passion, maintaining balance is not just an option—it is a necessity for long-term success and fulfillment. As Dabin continues to evolve as an artist, she remains committed to finding harmony in her life, ensuring that both her personal and professional worlds thrive in tandem.

Conquering the World: International Tours and Recognition

Expanding Horizons: Breaking into Global Markets

In the dynamic landscape of the music industry, the journey of *Neon Frequencies* from local sensations to global superstars epitomizes the essence of breaking into international markets. As the band sought to expand their horizons, they encountered a myriad of challenges and opportunities that shaped their path.

Understanding Global Markets

To successfully penetrate global markets, *Neon Frequencies* first needed to understand the cultural and economic landscapes of various regions. This involved extensive research into music consumption patterns, audience demographics, and regional preferences. For instance, they discovered that in countries like South Korea and Brazil, there was a growing appetite for genres that blended electronic, pop, and local musical influences.

$$\text{Market Penetration Rate} = \frac{\text{Number of New Fans}}{\text{Total Target Audience}} \times 100 \qquad (53)$$

This formula became a crucial metric for the band as they strategized their marketing efforts in foreign territories. By analyzing their market penetration rate, they could assess the effectiveness of their campaigns and adjust their approaches accordingly.

Collaborative Ventures

One of the pivotal strategies employed by *Neon Frequencies* was the formation of collaborations with international artists. This not only broadened their audience base but also enriched their musical repertoire. For example, collaborating with a renowned Brazilian artist allowed them to fuse their signature sound with traditional samba rhythms, creating a unique track that resonated well with both existing fans and new listeners.

Cultural Adaptation

Cultural adaptation played a significant role in *Neon Frequencies'* success in global markets. This involved not just altering their musical style but also understanding and respecting cultural nuances. The band made a concerted effort to learn about the customs and preferences of the regions they were targeting. For instance, during their promotional tour in Japan, they incorporated local instruments and themes into their performances, which greatly enhanced their reception.

Challenges and Solutions

Despite their enthusiasm, *Neon Frequencies* faced several challenges in their quest for global expansion. One major problem was the language barrier. Many of their songs contained intricate lyrics that might not translate well into other languages, potentially losing their meaning and emotional impact. To tackle this, the band collaborated with local lyricists who could adapt their songs while preserving the original essence.

Moreover, navigating the complexities of international music laws and regulations posed another hurdle. Each country has its own copyright laws, distribution channels, and performance rights organizations. To address this, the band enlisted the help of international music lawyers and agents who specialized in global market entry strategies.

Utilizing Digital Platforms

In the digital age, social media and streaming platforms have become invaluable tools for artists looking to break into global markets. *Neon Frequencies* harnessed the power of platforms like Spotify, YouTube, and TikTok to reach audiences worldwide. Their marketing team developed targeted campaigns that utilized analytics to identify regions with the highest engagement, allowing for tailored content that resonated with specific audiences.

$$\text{Engagement Rate} = \frac{\text{Total Interactions}}{\text{Total Followers}} \times 100 \qquad (54)$$

By calculating their engagement rate, the band could evaluate the success of their digital marketing strategies and make data-driven decisions to enhance their global outreach.

Global Tours and Festivals

Participating in international music festivals was another strategic move for *Neon Frequencies*. Events like Coachella, Glastonbury, and Lollapalooza not only provided a platform to showcase their music but also allowed them to connect with global audiences. These festivals often attract diverse crowds, offering the band an opportunity to gain exposure and build a fanbase that transcends geographical boundaries.

The band also organized their own global tours, strategically planning stops in key markets. This approach allowed them to create memorable experiences for fans and solidify their presence in the international music scene.

Conclusion

The journey of *Neon Frequencies* in expanding into global markets illustrates the intricate interplay between cultural understanding, strategic collaborations, and innovative marketing. Their success serves as a testament to the importance of adaptability and resilience in the ever-evolving music industry. As they continue to break barriers and redefine their sound, *Neon Frequencies* stands as a beacon of inspiration for aspiring artists looking to make their mark on the world stage.

Collaborations with International Artists: Fusing Cultures

The musical landscape in the 21st century is characterized by an unprecedented level of global connectivity, allowing artists from diverse backgrounds to collaborate and create innovative sounds. Dabin and Neon Frequencies exemplify this trend, as their collaborations with international artists have not only enriched their musical repertoire but also fostered a cultural exchange that transcends borders.

The Importance of Cultural Exchange in Music

Cultural exchange in music involves the blending of different musical traditions, styles, and influences, resulting in a unique fusion that reflects the diversity of the artists involved. This phenomenon can be understood through the lens of *hybridity theory*, which posits that cultural identities are not fixed but rather fluid and dynamic, shaped by interactions across various contexts. In music, this manifests as the combination of genres, instrumentation, and lyrical themes from different cultures.

$$C = \sum_{i=1}^{n}(M_i \cdot W_i) \qquad (55)$$

Where: - C is the resultant cultural product, - M_i represents the musical elements from each collaborating artist, - W_i is the weight or significance of each musical element in the fusion.

This equation illustrates how the collaboration of artists from varied backgrounds can lead to a richer cultural product, as each contributes unique elements to the overall composition.

Dabin's Collaborations: A Case Study

Dabin's collaborations with international artists have been pivotal in broadening the sound of Neon Frequencies. One notable example is his partnership with the acclaimed Brazilian musician, Caetano Veloso. Their track, "Samba de Neon", is a vibrant amalgamation of electronic beats and traditional Brazilian samba rhythms. The song exemplifies how different musical traditions can coexist and create something entirely new.

$$S = E + B \qquad (56)$$

Where: - S is the synthesized sound, - E represents electronic elements introduced by Dabin, - B is the traditional Brazilian rhythm.

This collaboration not only showcases the blending of genres but also highlights the importance of cross-cultural dialogue in music, as both artists bring their cultural narratives into the mix.

Challenges in Cross-Cultural Collaborations

While the fusion of cultures in music can lead to innovative and exciting outcomes, it is not without its challenges. One significant issue is the potential for *cultural appropriation*, where elements of one culture are used by artists from another culture without proper understanding or respect for their origins. This can lead to backlash from communities whose cultural heritage is being appropriated.

To mitigate this, Dabin and his bandmates have adopted a philosophy of *cultural sensitivity* and *collaborative authenticity*. This involves actively engaging with the cultural contexts of their collaborators and ensuring that the contributions of all artists are acknowledged and respected. For instance, during the recording of "Samba de Neon", Dabin and Veloso spent significant time discussing the historical and cultural significance of samba, ensuring that the final product honored its roots.

The Impact of International Collaborations on Neon Frequencies' Sound

The impact of these international collaborations is evident in the evolution of Neon Frequencies' sound. By integrating diverse musical elements, Dabin has been able to push the boundaries of the band's genre, creating a distinctive style that resonates with a global audience. This approach not only expands their listener base but also fosters a sense of unity among fans from different cultural backgrounds.

For example, the track "Echoes of the World", featuring Indian sitar virtuoso Anoushka Shankar, combines electronic music with traditional Indian classical music. The result is a mesmerizing soundscape that highlights the beauty of cultural fusion.

$$R = \alpha(E) + \beta(I) \qquad (57)$$

Where: - R is the resultant sound, - E represents electronic influences, - I is the Indian classical elements, - α and β are coefficients representing the degree of influence from each genre.

This equation reflects how the interplay between different musical styles can lead to the creation of a sound that is both innovative and reflective of multiple cultural identities.

Conclusion

In conclusion, Dabin's collaborations with international artists serve as a testament to the power of music as a unifying force. By embracing cultural exchange and navigating the complexities of cross-cultural collaborations, Neon Frequencies has not only enriched their sound but also contributed to a broader dialogue about identity, heritage, and creativity in the global music scene. The fusion of cultures in music is not just an artistic endeavor; it is a celebration of diversity and a reminder of our shared humanity. As Dabin continues to explore new musical landscapes, the future of Neon Frequencies promises to be as vibrant and eclectic as the cultures they represent.

Neon Frequencies' Global Impact: Inspiring Music Worldwide

Neon Frequencies, a name that resonates with the vibrant pulse of contemporary music, has not only captivated audiences but also significantly influenced the global music landscape. The band's eclectic sound, characterized by a fusion of genres, has transcended geographical boundaries, inspiring a new generation of musicians and fans alike. This section delves into the myriad ways in which Neon Frequencies has left an indelible mark on the world of music.

Cultural Fusion and Genre Blending

One of the hallmarks of Neon Frequencies is their ability to blend diverse musical genres, creating a unique sound that appeals to a broad audience. This genre-blending approach can be analyzed through the lens of cultural fusion, where musical elements from different traditions are combined to create something entirely new. For instance, the incorporation of electronic beats with traditional acoustic instruments has not only broadened their appeal but has also encouraged other artists to experiment with similar blends.

The equation for cultural fusion in music can be represented as follows:

$$C = \sum_{i=1}^{n}(G_i \times E_i) \qquad (58)$$

Where: - C is the cultural fusion outcome, - G_i represents the genre influences, - E_i represents the emotional impact of each genre.

This equation illustrates how Neon Frequencies has successfully harnessed the emotional resonance of various genres to create music that speaks to the heart and soul of listeners around the world.

Inspiring Emerging Artists

Neon Frequencies' success story has served as a beacon of hope for aspiring musicians globally. Their journey from local performers to international superstars exemplifies the potential for creativity and hard work to break barriers. Many emerging artists cite Neon Frequencies as a source of inspiration, often emulating their innovative spirit and willingness to push musical boundaries.

For example, artists from countries such as Brazil, South Korea, and Nigeria have incorporated elements of Neon Frequencies' sound into their own music, leading to a rich tapestry of global music that reflects a shared cultural experience. This phenomenon can be observed in the rise of genres like Afrobeats and K-Pop, which have started to embrace electronic influences, showcasing the ripple effect of Neon Frequencies' musical approach.

Global Collaborations and Cross-Cultural Exchange

The band's commitment to collaboration has further amplified their global impact. By partnering with artists from various cultural backgrounds, Neon Frequencies has fostered a spirit of cross-cultural exchange. These collaborations not only enhance their musical repertoire but also promote understanding and appreciation of diverse musical traditions.

A notable example of this is their collaboration with Afrobeat artist Femi Kuti. The resulting track not only topped charts in multiple countries but also introduced fans to the rich heritage of Afrobeat, thus bridging cultural divides. This collaborative spirit can be represented by the following model:

$$I = \sum_{j=1}^{m}(C_j \times R_j) \qquad (59)$$

Where: - I is the impact of collaboration, - C_j represents the cultural elements introduced, - R_j represents the reach of each collaborative effort.

Through this model, it is evident that the cultural elements introduced by Neon Frequencies through collaborations significantly enhance their global reach and impact.

Social Media and the Digital Age

In the age of digital connectivity, Neon Frequencies has adeptly utilized social media platforms to engage with a worldwide audience. Their strategic use of platforms such as Instagram, Twitter, and TikTok has not only amplified their music but has also fostered a global community of fans. The viral nature of social media has allowed their music to reach regions previously untouched by their genre, further solidifying their global presence.

The influence of social media on their global impact can be quantified using the following equation:

$$S = \frac{E \times R}{T} \quad (60)$$

Where: - S is the social impact, - E is the engagement rate, - R is the reach of their content, - T is the time taken for the content to go viral.

This equation underscores the importance of timely and engaging content in maximizing their global influence.

Legacy and Future Directions

As Neon Frequencies continues to evolve, their legacy as a source of inspiration for musicians worldwide remains firmly entrenched. The band's commitment to innovation and cultural exchange sets a precedent for future artists to follow. Their impact is not merely confined to music; it extends to social movements, advocating for inclusivity and diversity within the music industry.

In conclusion, Neon Frequencies' global impact is a testament to the power of music as a unifying force. By inspiring emerging artists, fostering cultural fusion, and leveraging the digital landscape, they have not only carved out a niche for themselves but have also paved the way for future generations of musicians. The journey of Neon Frequencies is far from over, and as they continue to inspire, the world eagerly awaits the next chapter in their extraordinary story.

Leaving a Legacy

The Influence on Future Generations of Musicians

The legacy of Neon Frequencies, particularly through the creative genius of Dabin, has left an indelible mark on the landscape of modern music. This influence can be observed in several dimensions, including stylistic innovations, collaborative practices, and the cultivation of a dedicated fanbase. As we delve into the specifics, it is essential to recognize how these elements have shaped the aspirations and methodologies of emerging artists.

Stylistic Innovations

Dabin's unique sound, characterized by an eclectic fusion of genres, has inspired countless musicians to experiment beyond traditional boundaries. The blending of electronic elements with organic instrumentation has become a hallmark of contemporary music, encouraging new artists to explore their sonic identities. For instance, the incorporation of *vocal chops*, a technique popularized by Dabin, has been widely adopted in various genres, from pop to hip-hop. This technique involves slicing and rearranging vocal samples to create rhythmic and melodic patterns, thus expanding the creative toolkit available to budding musicians.

$$V_c = \sum_{i=1}^{n} a_i \cdot f_i(t) \tag{61}$$

where V_c represents the resultant vocal chop, a_i are the amplitude coefficients of the chopped samples, and $f_i(t)$ denotes the frequency function of each sample over time t.

The influence of Neon Frequencies can also be seen in the rise of *genre-blending* artists who draw from multiple influences to create their distinctive sounds. For example, artists like *Grimes* and *Flume* have cited Dabin's work as pivotal in their musical development, illustrating how the band's innovative approach has permeated the creative processes of future generations.

Collaborative Practices

The collaborative spirit that Neon Frequencies embodied has set a precedent for modern musicians. Dabin's partnerships with various artists across genres have highlighted the importance of collaboration in fostering creativity and innovation.

This is particularly evident in the rise of *collaborative albums* and *cross-genre projects*, where artists come together to create works that transcend their individual styles.

For example, the project *"Collab 2023"*, which features a diverse array of artists from different musical backgrounds, showcases how Dabin's influence has encouraged musicians to step outside their comfort zones. This collaborative ethos not only enriches the music itself but also promotes a sense of community among artists, fostering an environment where experimentation is celebrated.

Cultivating a Dedicated Fanbase

Neon Frequencies' ability to engage and cultivate a passionate fanbase has become a blueprint for aspiring musicians. The band's emphasis on direct interaction with fans through social media, live performances, and fan events has set a standard for artist-fan relationships in the digital age. This engagement has led to the emergence of what can be termed as *fan culture*, where dedicated followers actively participate in the promotion and celebration of their favorite artists.

Emerging musicians have taken cues from this model, employing platforms like Instagram, TikTok, and YouTube to build their own communities. The success of artists such as *Olivia Rodrigo* and *Lil Nas X* can be attributed in part to their savvy use of social media to connect with fans, echoing the practices established by Neon Frequencies.

Educational Impact

Moreover, Dabin's influence extends into the realm of music education. Many music programs now incorporate the study of genre-blending techniques and the use of technology in music production, reflecting the innovative approaches that Neon Frequencies championed. Workshops, seminars, and online courses often feature modules dedicated to understanding the band's impact on modern music, illustrating how their legacy continues to shape the next generation of musicians.

Conclusion

In conclusion, the influence of Neon Frequencies, particularly through Dabin's artistic vision, has catalyzed a transformation in how future generations of musicians approach their craft. From stylistic innovations and collaborative practices to the cultivation of dedicated fanbases, the band's legacy serves as a guiding light for aspiring artists. As they navigate the ever-evolving music landscape, the lessons learned from Neon Frequencies will undoubtedly resonate, inspiring creativity, collaboration, and a profound connection to their audiences.

The journey of music is an infinite loop, and as new artists rise, they carry forward the torch lit by pioneers like Dabin and Neon Frequencies, ensuring that their influence will echo through the corridors of music history for years to come.

Using Stardom for Good: Dabin's Philanthropic Endeavors

As Dabin's star ascended in the music industry, she harnessed her fame to champion various philanthropic causes, demonstrating that stardom could transcend mere entertainment and serve as a powerful vehicle for positive change. This section delves into the impactful philanthropic endeavors spearheaded by Dabin, illustrating her commitment to using her platform for the greater good.

The Philosophy of Giving Back

Dabin's journey into philanthropy is rooted in a profound understanding of her influence. Acknowledging the privilege that comes with fame, she adopted the philosophy that with great power comes great responsibility. This sentiment echoes the sentiments of many artists who believe that their visibility can amplify voices and issues that might otherwise go unheard.

$$\text{Impact} = \text{Visibility} \times \text{Awareness} \tag{62}$$

Where Impact represents the change initiated by philanthropic efforts, Visibility is the celebrity's reach, and Awareness reflects the public's understanding of the cause. Dabin recognized that her visibility could be leveraged to raise awareness about critical social issues, ultimately leading to impactful outcomes.

Key Initiatives and Collaborations

Dabin's philanthropic journey began with her involvement in local charities during her formative years. However, as her fame grew, so did the scale of her initiatives. Some of her most notable philanthropic endeavors include:

- **Music for Change:** In 2020, Dabin launched the "Music for Change" initiative, which aimed to provide music education to underprivileged youth. The program offered free workshops, instruments, and mentorship from established musicians. The initiative not only nurtured young talent but also fostered a sense of community and belonging among participants.

- **Health and Wellness Campaigns:** Dabin partnered with various health organizations to promote mental health awareness, particularly among young people. Her campaign, "Voices Matter," utilized social media platforms to share personal stories of struggle and resilience, encouraging fans to seek help and support. This initiative highlighted the importance of mental health, particularly in the high-pressure environment of the music industry.

- **Environmental Advocacy:** Recognizing the urgency of climate change, Dabin became an advocate for environmental sustainability. She collaborated with environmental organizations to promote eco-friendly practices within the music industry, including reducing plastic waste at concerts and encouraging fans to participate in local clean-up efforts. Her single "Green Beats" was released with proceeds going directly to environmental charities.

Challenges and Criticisms

Despite her noble intentions, Dabin faced challenges in her philanthropic endeavors. Critics often pointed out that celebrity-led initiatives could sometimes lack depth or sustainability. For instance, the "Music for Change" initiative initially struggled with funding and outreach, leading to questions about its long-term viability.

To address these concerns, Dabin implemented a feedback loop, incorporating insights from participants and local communities to refine and enhance her programs. This approach not only improved the effectiveness of her initiatives but also fostered a sense of ownership among beneficiaries.

The Ripple Effect of Philanthropy

Dabin's commitment to philanthropy has created a ripple effect within the music industry and beyond. By openly discussing her charitable efforts, she has inspired fellow artists to engage in their own philanthropic pursuits. Collaborations with other musicians for charity singles and benefit concerts have become more prevalent, creating a culture of giving within the industry.

$$\text{Cultural Shift} = \text{Artist Engagement} + \text{Public Participation} \qquad (63)$$

Where Cultural Shift represents the broader movement towards philanthropy in the music industry, Artist Engagement reflects the involvement of musicians in charitable activities, and Public Participation denotes the support and involvement of fans and the general public.

Legacy and Continuing Impact

As Dabin continues her journey, her philanthropic endeavors remain a cornerstone of her identity as an artist. She understands that her legacy will not solely be defined by her music but also by the positive change she has inspired. Dabin's commitment to philanthropy has not only benefited countless individuals but has also set a precedent for future generations of artists.

In conclusion, Dabin's philanthropic endeavors exemplify the profound impact a celebrity can have on society. By leveraging her fame for good, she has become a beacon of hope and inspiration, proving that music can be a powerful catalyst for change. Her story serves as a reminder that every artist has the potential to make a difference, and that true stardom lies in the ability to uplift others.

Reflecting on the Journey: Lessons Learned and Wisdom Gained

As the curtain begins to close on the vibrant saga of Neon Frequencies, it's essential to pause and reflect on the myriad lessons learned throughout the journey. The road traveled has been paved with both triumphs and tribulations, each contributing to the rich tapestry of experiences that define Dabin and the band. This reflection is not just a look back; it serves as a compass for future endeavors, illuminating the wisdom gained through years of artistry, collaboration, and personal growth.

The Importance of Authenticity

One of the most profound lessons learned is the significance of authenticity in music. In an industry often driven by trends and marketability, Dabin and her bandmates discovered that staying true to their artistic vision was paramount. The realization that genuine expression resonates more deeply with audiences than mere commercial appeal became a guiding principle. This authenticity is reflected in their music, which blends personal narratives with universal themes, creating a connection that transcends the superficiality often found in pop culture.

Embracing Vulnerability

The journey of Neon Frequencies also highlighted the power of vulnerability. Sharing personal stories through music requires courage, as it opens the door to criticism and scrutiny. However, Dabin learned that embracing vulnerability not only fosters deeper connections with fans but also leads to personal healing and growth. Songs like "Echoes of Yesterday" exemplify this, where raw emotions are laid bare, inviting listeners to share in the experience. This lesson in vulnerability has encouraged Dabin to continue exploring her emotions and experiences, transforming them into art that resonates on a profound level.

The Value of Collaboration

Collaboration emerged as a cornerstone of success for Neon Frequencies. The chemistry among bandmates played a crucial role in shaping their sound and identity. The diverse backgrounds and influences brought by each member enriched the creative process, leading to innovative musical explorations. Dabin learned that collaboration extends beyond the band; working with producers, songwriters, and even fans has the potential to elevate a project. This collective effort fosters an environment where creativity flourishes, resulting in a sound that is greater than the sum of its parts.

Resilience in the Face of Adversity

The music industry is fraught with challenges, from creative differences to the pressures of fame. Throughout their journey, Dabin and the band faced numerous obstacles that tested their resilience. Learning to navigate these challenges has been instrumental in their growth. For instance, during the recording of their second album, the band encountered significant creative disagreements. Instead of allowing these conflicts to fracture their unity, they embraced open communication and compromise, ultimately leading to a stronger, more cohesive sound. This experience taught them that resilience is not merely about enduring hardship but also about adapting and evolving in the face of it.

The Impact of Community

Another critical lesson learned is the importance of community. The support of fans, family, and fellow musicians has been invaluable throughout the journey. Dabin realized that music is not created in isolation; it thrives within a community that shares a passion for art. Engaging with their fanbase through social media, meet-and-greets, and live performances has fostered a sense of belonging that fuels their creativity. This connection with fans has not only provided emotional support but has also inspired new ideas and collaborations, reinforcing the idea that community is an essential ingredient in the creative process.

Legacy and Responsibility

As Neon Frequencies reflects on their journey, the concept of legacy weighs heavily on their minds. Dabin understands that with success comes responsibility—the responsibility to inspire future generations of musicians and to use their platform for good. This awareness has led her to engage in philanthropic endeavors, using her music to advocate for causes close to her heart. The realization that their art can impact lives beyond the stage has instilled a sense of purpose, motivating Dabin to continue pushing boundaries and exploring new horizons.

Conclusion

In conclusion, the journey of Neon Frequencies has been a profound learning experience, filled with lessons that transcend the realm of music. From the importance of authenticity and vulnerability to the value of collaboration and community, Dabin has emerged not only as an artist but also as a mentor and advocate. As they prepare to step into the next chapter, the wisdom gained from their experiences will undoubtedly guide them, ensuring that the legacy of Neon Frequencies continues to inspire and resonate for years to come. The journey may evolve, but the lessons learned will remain etched in the heart of their music, echoing through time like the vibrant melodies that first brought them together.

The Final Act of Neon Frequencies

The Final Act of Neon Frequencies

The Final Act of Neon Frequencies

As the curtain begins to close on the vibrant saga of Neon Frequencies, we find ourselves at a poignant juncture—the final act of a mesmerizing journey that has captivated hearts and souls across the globe. This chapter delves into the bittersweet culmination of the band's legacy, exploring the emotional complexities of saying goodbye while celebrating the indelible mark they have left on the music industry.

The narrative of the final act is not merely about the end; it is a testament to the evolution, growth, and transformation that Neon Frequencies has undergone. The final album, aptly titled *A Farewell to Fans*, serves as a reflective encapsulation of their journey. It is a collection of songs that resonate with themes of nostalgia, triumph, and introspection, inviting listeners to reminisce about the moments that defined the band's trajectory.

The creative process behind this last album is steeped in emotion. Each band member brought their unique experiences and perspectives, creating a rich tapestry of sound that reflects their collective journey. The songwriting sessions were marked by collaboration and camaraderie, as they sought to capture the essence of their shared experiences while acknowledging the inevitability of change. This process not only solidified their bond but also highlighted the challenges of balancing individual artistic visions with the cohesive identity of the band.

$$S = \sum_{i=1}^{n} s_i \tag{64}$$

Where S represents the final sound of the album, and s_i denotes the individual contributions from each band member. This equation symbolizes the synergy that emerges when diverse talents unite to create something greater than the sum of its parts.

The farewell tour, a series of sold-out shows across iconic venues, became a celebration of their journey. Each performance was infused with emotion, as fans and bandmates alike reflected on the memories forged over the years. The energy in the air was palpable; it was a collective acknowledgment of the impact Neon Frequencies had on their lives. The final concert, an unforgettable night, was not just a performance but a ritual of closure, a moment where past and present converged in a euphoric celebration of music.

Throughout this chapter, we explore the intricate dynamics within the band as they navigated the complexities of their final act. The emotional weight of their decision to part ways was not lost on any member. Creative differences surfaced, yet they were met with understanding and respect. This chapter highlights how the band members learned to embrace these differences, recognizing them as essential to their growth both as individuals and as a collective.

In the aftermath of their farewell tour, the landscape of music continued to evolve, but the legacy of Neon Frequencies remained etched in the hearts of fans worldwide. Their influence transcended genres and generations, inspiring countless musicians to pursue their dreams. As we reflect on the final act, we acknowledge the profound impact of their music—an impact that will resonate long after the last note has faded.

In conclusion, Chapter 4 encapsulates not just the end of an era but the enduring spirit of Neon Frequencies. Their journey is a reminder that while all good things must come to an end, the echoes of their music will continue to inspire and uplift, a testament to the power of creativity, collaboration, and the unbreakable bonds of friendship.

The Last Album: A Farewell to Fans

Creating a Testament to the Band's Musical Evolution

As Neon Frequencies approached the creation of their final album, the members found themselves at a pivotal crossroads—a moment that would not only encapsulate their musical journey but also serve as a testament to their evolution as artists. This section delves into the intricate process of crafting an album that reflects their growth, challenges, and the essence of their sound.

The Conceptual Framework

The first step in this creative endeavor was establishing a conceptual framework that would guide the album's direction. The band convened in a series of brainstorming sessions, fueled by both nostalgia and ambition. They recognized that their music had evolved significantly since their inception, and this album needed to capture that trajectory.

To articulate their vision, the band members utilized a theoretical model based on the *Four Stages of Musical Evolution*, which posits that every artist undergoes a cycle of experimentation, refinement, innovation, and legacy. This model served as a roadmap for their songwriting process:

$$\text{Musical Evolution} = \text{Experimentation} + \text{Refinement} + \text{Innovation} + \text{Legacy} \quad (65)$$

Each stage was reflected in the songs they crafted, allowing them to explore new sounds while honoring their roots.

Thematic Depth and Lyrical Content

In parallel with the musical structure, the band focused on thematic depth and lyrical content. Dabin, as the primary lyricist, drew inspiration from personal experiences, relationships, and the collective memory of the band. This introspective approach was pivotal in shaping the album's narrative arc.

The band decided to incorporate recurring motifs that symbolized their journey, such as:

- **Resilience:** Lyrics that reflect overcoming obstacles, symbolizing their struggles and triumphs.

- **Unity:** Themes of camaraderie and collaboration, celebrating the bond that formed the backbone of Neon Frequencies.

- **Reflection:** Introspective lyrics that encourage listeners to contemplate their own journeys, mirroring the band's evolution.

By weaving these motifs throughout the album, they aimed to create a cohesive narrative that resonated with their audience.

Collaborative Songwriting Sessions

To enhance the creative process, the band engaged in collaborative songwriting sessions, where each member contributed their unique perspectives and talents. This approach not only fostered a sense of unity but also allowed for a rich exchange of ideas.

During these sessions, they employed a method known as *Collaborative Improvisation*, where they would jam together, capturing spontaneous musical ideas. These sessions often led to unexpected breakthroughs, resulting in tracks that embodied the band's multifaceted sound.

For instance, one memorable session resulted in the song "Elysium," which seamlessly blended electronic elements with acoustic instrumentation, showcasing their willingness to push boundaries. The creative synergy during these moments was palpable, as they collectively embraced the spirit of experimentation.

Incorporating Feedback and Iteration

As the album took shape, the band sought feedback from trusted collaborators and industry veterans. This external input was invaluable in refining their sound and ensuring that the album resonated with their audience.

The iterative process involved revisiting songs based on feedback, making adjustments to melodies, harmonies, and arrangements. For example, the track "Echoes of Tomorrow" underwent several revisions, transforming from a simple ballad into an anthemic piece that captured the essence of hope and resilience.

Through this feedback loop, they embraced the idea that evolution is not a linear path but rather a dynamic process that requires adaptability and openness to change.

Finalizing the Album: A Testament to Growth

As the recording sessions progressed, the band found themselves reflecting on their journey. Each track became a chapter in their story, showcasing their growth as musicians and individuals. They recognized that this album was not just a farewell but a celebration of their legacy.

In the final stages of production, they crafted a closing track titled "A New Dawn," which encapsulated the essence of their musical evolution. The song served as a bridge between their past and future, inviting listeners to join them on a journey of reflection and hope.

Ultimately, the album emerged as a testament to the band's musical evolution—an intricate tapestry woven from their experiences, challenges, and triumphs. It stood as a reminder that while their time as Neon Frequencies was coming to an end, their legacy would continue to inspire future generations of musicians.

In conclusion, the creation of this album was not merely about producing music; it was about encapsulating a journey that spanned years of growth, experimentation, and connection. The process of crafting a testament to their evolution was a profound experience that enriched not only their artistic expression but also their relationships with one another and their fans.

Reflections on the Band's Journey: Triumphs, Regrets, and Growth

The journey of Neon Frequencies has been nothing short of a rollercoaster ride, marked by exhilarating highs and poignant lows. As the band prepares to bid farewell to their fans, it is essential to reflect on the myriad experiences that have shaped their musical legacy. This section delves into the triumphs that propelled them to stardom, the regrets that linger in the shadows, and the profound growth that has emerged from their collective journey.

Triumphs: Celebrating Successes

From their inception, Neon Frequencies has achieved remarkable milestones that have solidified their place in the music industry. The band's first major triumph came with the release of their debut album, which not only topped charts but also resonated deeply with fans. The fusion of genres and innovative sound captured the essence of a generation, leading to accolades such as *Best New Artist* at major music awards.

One of the most significant triumphs was their sold-out world tour, which showcased their electrifying live performances. Each concert was a celebration of their journey, where fans sang along to every lyric, creating an atmosphere of unity and euphoria. The chemistry between band members on stage was palpable, resulting in unforgettable moments that solidified their reputation as a must-see live act.

The band's ability to connect with their audience through social media also contributed to their success. By engaging with fans directly, they cultivated a loyal following that extended beyond geographical boundaries. This connection not only amplified their reach but also fostered a sense of community among listeners, further enhancing their impact on the music scene.

Regrets: Lessons Learned

Despite the glitz and glamour of their journey, Neon Frequencies faced challenges that led to moments of regret. One notable regret was the internal conflicts that arose during the creative process. As artistic visions clashed, tensions mounted, and the collaborative spirit that initially defined the band began to fray. This discord not only affected their songwriting but also strained personal relationships within the group.

Additionally, the pressures of fame took a toll on the members' mental health. The relentless schedule of touring and recording often left little room for self-care, leading to burnout and exhaustion. In retrospect, the band recognizes the importance of prioritizing mental well-being, acknowledging that a healthier balance could have mitigated some of the challenges they faced.

The loss of connection with their roots also stands out as a regret. As the band ascended to stardom, they found themselves distanced from the intimate, grassroots performances that initially fueled their passion. Reflecting on this, the members express a desire to return to those humble beginnings, where music was created for the sheer joy of it, rather than the pressures of commercial success.

Growth: Evolving Through Experience

Through the triumphs and regrets, Neon Frequencies has experienced profound growth both as individuals and as a band. Each challenge faced has served as a catalyst for personal development, fostering resilience and adaptability. The members have learned to communicate more openly, embracing constructive criticism and valuing each other's perspectives. This evolution has strengthened their bond, resulting in a more cohesive and harmonious creative process.

Moreover, the band's exploration of different musical styles has enriched their sound, allowing them to push boundaries and redefine their artistic identity. Dabin's solo ventures, for instance, have influenced the band's direction, introducing new elements that resonate with their evolving fan base. This willingness to experiment has not only kept their music fresh but has also showcased their versatility as artists.

As they reflect on their journey, the members of Neon Frequencies recognize the importance of using their platform for good. Engaging in philanthropic endeavors has become a significant aspect of their growth, as they aim to give back to the community that has supported them throughout their career. This commitment to social responsibility has not only deepened their connection with fans but has also instilled a sense of purpose beyond music.

In conclusion, the journey of Neon Frequencies is a tapestry woven with triumphs, regrets, and growth. As they prepare to release their final album and embark on their farewell tour, the band embraces the lessons learned along the way. Each experience has shaped their identity, leaving an indelible mark on their legacy. The reflections on their journey serve as a reminder that success is not solely defined by accolades, but by the connections forged, the lessons learned, and the growth experienced together.

Collaborations and Farewell Songwriting Sessions

As Neon Frequencies approached their final chapter, the band members found themselves reflecting on their journey, both as individuals and as a collective. The farewell songwriting sessions became a sacred space where creativity flourished, allowing each member to contribute their unique voice to the band's legacy. This section delves into the collaborative spirit that defined these sessions, the challenges they faced, and the magic that emerged from their combined efforts.

The Essence of Collaboration

Collaboration in music is often likened to a dance; it requires trust, rhythm, and an understanding of one another's strengths. For Dabin and the bandmates, this meant revisiting the chemistry that had initially ignited their sound. During these farewell sessions, they aimed to create songs that encapsulated their shared experiences, emotions, and the essence of what it meant to be part of Neon Frequencies.

The songwriting process was not without its challenges. Each member brought their own influences and ideas, which sometimes led to creative friction. However, it was precisely this tension that often birthed the most compelling music. As they navigated through differing perspectives, they employed a method known as *creative convergence*, where individual ideas were synthesized into a singular vision. This approach not only strengthened their bond but also enriched their musical palette.

Emotional Resonance in Farewell Songs

The emotional weight of creating farewell songs cannot be overstated. The band members were acutely aware that these tracks would serve as a final testament to their journey together. They focused on themes of nostalgia, gratitude, and closure. For instance, one of the standout tracks, titled *"Echoes of Tomorrow"*, was born out of a late-night jam session. The lyrics reflected on the memories they had created, encapsulating both the highs and lows of their experiences.

The songwriting process involved a blend of introspection and collaboration. Dabin often took the lead in crafting melodies that resonated with the emotional themes they were exploring. To illustrate, the chord progression for *"Echoes of Tomorrow"* can be expressed mathematically as follows:

$$C - G - Am - F \tag{66}$$

This progression, a staple in pop music, evokes a sense of longing and warmth, perfectly aligning with the song's lyrical content. The band utilized this familiar structure while infusing it with their signature sound, creating a bridge between their past and future.

The Role of Guest Collaborators

To enrich their farewell album, Neon Frequencies invited several guest artists to join their final songwriting sessions. These collaborations not only added fresh perspectives but also honored the friendships they had forged throughout their career. One notable collaboration was with the acclaimed artist *Luna Ray*, whose ethereal vocals complemented Dabin's signature sound beautifully.

During their collaborative sessions, the band and Luna explored the concept of *musical intertextuality*, where they drew inspiration from each other's works. This is exemplified in the track *"Fading Stars"*, which blended elements of Luna's folk influences with Neon Frequencies' electronic roots. The result was a rich tapestry of sound that resonated deeply with both their fanbases.

The Final Songwriting Retreat

In a bid to encapsulate their journey, the band organized a final songwriting retreat in a secluded cabin in the mountains. This retreat served as a sanctuary for creativity, allowing them to disconnect from the pressures of the outside world. Surrounded by nature, they found inspiration in the serene environment, which influenced the tone of their final tracks.

During this retreat, the band engaged in a unique exercise known as *musical storytelling*. They would take turns sharing personal anecdotes from their time together, which would then be transformed into lyrical themes. This process not only fostered a deeper connection among the members but also ensured that their final songs were imbued with authenticity.

Challenges Faced During the Farewell Sessions

While the farewell songwriting sessions were filled with creativity and camaraderie, they were not without challenges. The emotional weight of saying goodbye often led to moments of vulnerability among the band members. Some struggled with the idea of closure, while others grappled with the fear of stepping into the unknown.

To address these challenges, the band established a supportive environment where open communication was encouraged. They implemented regular check-ins, allowing each member to express their feelings and concerns. This practice not only strengthened their bond but also facilitated a healthier creative process.

The Legacy of the Farewell Album

The culmination of their collaborative efforts resulted in the farewell album, aptly titled *"Lasting Frequencies"*. This album not only serves as a musical farewell but also as a legacy for future generations of musicians. Each track is a reflection of their journey, encapsulating the essence of Neon Frequencies.

The album's lead single, *"A New Dawn"*, became an anthem for fans, celebrating both the end of an era and the promise of new beginnings. The chorus, characterized by soaring melodies and heartfelt lyrics, resonates with listeners, reminding them that every ending is merely a prelude to a new chapter.

In conclusion, the farewell songwriting sessions of Neon Frequencies were a profound exploration of creativity, collaboration, and emotional resonance. Through their collective efforts, they crafted an album that not only honors their past but also inspires future musicians to embrace the power of collaboration and storytelling in their own journeys.

The Farewell Tour: An Emotional Goodbye

Sold-Out Shows and Farewell Performances

As Neon Frequencies approached the culmination of their illustrious journey, the anticipation surrounding their farewell performances reached a fever pitch. Fans from all corners of the globe clamored for tickets, resulting in a series of sold-out shows that would go down in history as some of the most electrifying moments in the band's career. The atmosphere was charged with emotion, nostalgia, and a palpable sense of community, as fans united to celebrate the music that had soundtracked their lives.

The Phenomenon of Sold-Out Shows

Sold-out shows are not merely a testament to a band's popularity; they signify a deep connection between the artists and their audience. This phenomenon can be analyzed through the lens of social psychology, where the concept of **collective effervescence** plays a critical role. According to Durkheim's theory, collective effervescence refers to the energy and excitement generated when individuals come together in a shared experience, such as a live concert. This shared emotional experience fosters a sense of belonging and unity, making each sold-out performance a celebration of not only the band's music but also the fans' loyalty and passion.

$$P = \frac{N}{T} \qquad (67)$$

Where:

- P = Probability of a sold-out show
- N = Number of tickets sold
- T = Total number of tickets available

As Neon Frequencies prepared for their farewell tour, the probability of sold-out shows increased dramatically, with numerous venues experiencing ticket sales that surpassed expectations. The excitement surrounding the band's final performances was palpable, as fans shared their experiences on social media, creating a buzz that further fueled demand.

Setting the Stage for Farewell Performances

The farewell performances were meticulously crafted to create an unforgettable experience for fans. Each venue was transformed into a visual spectacle, featuring elaborate stage designs that reflected the band's journey and evolution. The integration of cutting-edge technology, such as immersive light shows and high-definition visuals, added a layer of depth to the performances, ensuring that every moment was a feast for the senses.

The setlist was a carefully curated selection of the band's greatest hits, interspersed with fan favorites and unreleased tracks. The choice of songs was not only a nod to the band's past but also a way to acknowledge the emotional connection fans had with each piece. This strategic selection can be understood through the **Nostalgia Theory**, which posits that individuals derive comfort and joy from reminiscing about the past. By including beloved tracks, the band tapped into the emotional reservoir of their audience, creating a powerful and nostalgic atmosphere.

The Emotional Impact of Farewell Shows

Each sold-out performance was imbued with an emotional weight that transcended the music itself. As the final notes of their last song echoed through the venues, the audience was left in a state of collective reflection. Tears flowed, laughter erupted, and heartfelt tributes were exchanged between fans and band members alike. The emotional impact of these farewell performances can be analyzed through the **Cognitive Appraisal Theory**, which suggests that individuals evaluate emotional experiences based on personal significance. For many fans, these performances represented not only a farewell to a beloved band but also a closure to a significant chapter in their lives.

$$E = f(C, A) \tag{68}$$

Where:

- E = Emotional experience
- C = Context of the performance
- A = Audience's personal appraisal

The combination of the band's context—performing their last shows—and the audience's personal appraisals of the music created a potent emotional experience that resonated deeply with everyone present.

Memorable Moments and Highlights

The farewell performances were punctuated by memorable moments that would be etched in the minds of fans forever. Special guest appearances, surprise acoustic sets, and heartfelt speeches from band members added layers of intimacy to the shows. One particularly poignant moment occurred during the final concert, where the band dedicated a song to their fans, expressing gratitude for their unwavering support throughout the years. This act of acknowledgment not only solidified the bond between the band and their audience but also served as a reminder of the shared journey they had embarked upon together.

The power of these farewell performances extended beyond the concert halls. Fans shared their experiences on social media platforms, creating a digital tapestry of memories that would live on long after the last note had faded. Hashtags like #FarewellNeonFrequencies and #ForeverInOurHearts trended worldwide, illustrating the profound impact the band had on their fans' lives.

In conclusion, the sold-out shows and farewell performances of Neon Frequencies were more than just concerts; they were a celebration of a remarkable journey that had touched the hearts of many. The emotional connections forged, the memories created, and the legacy left behind would continue to resonate long after the curtain fell. As the lights dimmed for the final time, the spirit of Neon Frequencies lived on in the hearts of their devoted fans, immortalized in the music that had brought them together.

Bittersweet Memories on the Road: Celebrating the Journey

As the final tour of Neon Frequencies unfolded, the band found themselves navigating a landscape rich with nostalgia and emotion. Each city visited was a chapter in their shared story, filled with laughter, challenges, and unforgettable moments. The bittersweet nature of this journey was not lost on the band members, who were acutely aware that each performance was not just a show, but a celebration of their collective experiences.

The road had been paved with memories, each venue echoing with the sounds of past performances. From the intimate settings of small clubs to the electrifying atmosphere of packed stadiums, every location held a piece of their history. The band reminisced about their first gig at a local café, where they performed to a handful of friends and curious patrons. The thrill of that night was palpable, as they felt the spark of something special beginning to ignite.

$$\text{Joy} = \frac{\text{Memories}}{\text{Time}} \times \text{Nostalgia} \qquad (69)$$

This equation encapsulates the essence of their experiences on the road. Joy was derived not just from the memories created, but from the passage of time that allowed those memories to deepen in significance. Nostalgia played a crucial role, amplifying the emotional weight of each recollection.

During the farewell tour, the band members often shared stories from their travels, recounting hilarious mishaps, late-night escapades, and the bonds forged through shared adversity. One memorable incident involved a van breakdown in the middle of nowhere, which led to an impromptu jam session by the roadside, transforming a frustrating situation into a cherished memory. The camaraderie that emerged from such experiences highlighted the profound connections that had developed over the years.

THE FAREWELL TOUR: AN EMOTIONAL GOODBYE

$$\text{Connection} = \text{Shared Experiences} + \text{Adversity} \tag{70}$$

This equation illustrates how connections among band members were strengthened through shared experiences, particularly during challenging times. The ability to laugh and create together, even in the face of adversity, was a testament to their resilience and friendship.

As the tour progressed, the band dedicated moments in their setlist to reflect on their journey. They would often pause between songs to share heartfelt anecdotes with the audience, inviting fans into their world and allowing them to feel the weight of the moment. These interactions fostered a sense of community, as fans resonated with the stories of struggle and triumph. The energy in the venues shifted, transforming from mere spectatorship to an immersive experience where everyone felt like part of the Neon Frequencies family.

$$\text{Audience Engagement} = \text{Storytelling} + \text{Emotional Connection} \tag{71}$$

This equation emphasizes the importance of storytelling in enhancing audience engagement. By sharing their personal narratives, the band cultivated emotional connections that transcended the music itself, creating a shared experience that would linger long after the final note was played.

The farewell tour also served as a reminder of the ephemeral nature of their journey. Each concert was tinged with the realization that this was a culmination of years of hard work, dedication, and passion. The bittersweet emotions were palpable as they took the stage for the last time in various cities, knowing that they were saying goodbye not just to the fans, but to a significant chapter of their lives.

In the final moments of each concert, as the last chords reverberated through the air, the band members would often look at each other with a mix of pride and sorrow. They knew they had given their all, and the memories created would forever be etched in their hearts. The audience would erupt in applause, a beautiful cacophony of appreciation that echoed their shared journey.

$$\text{Legacy} = \text{Impact on Fans} + \text{Cultural Significance} \tag{72}$$

This equation captures the essence of the band's legacy. The impact they had on their fans and the cultural significance of their music would resonate long after the final tour ended. As Neon Frequencies bid farewell, they left behind a treasure trove of memories, experiences, and a legacy that would inspire future generations of musicians and fans alike.

In conclusion, the farewell tour was not merely an end; it was a celebration of everything that Neon Frequencies had accomplished together. The bittersweet memories forged on the road served as a testament to their journey, a reminder that every ending is also a new beginning. As they stepped off the stage for the last time, the echoes of their music and the love of their fans lingered in the air, a beautiful reminder of the magic they had created together.

The Last Concert: A Night of Nostalgia and Celebration

As the lights dimmed and the crowd's anticipation reached a fever pitch, the atmosphere was electric with a sense of finality and joy. The last concert of *Neon Frequencies* was not just a performance; it was a heartfelt celebration of years filled with music, memories, and the indelible mark they left on the hearts of their fans. The venue, a grand arena that had hosted countless iconic performances, felt like a sacred space where the echoes of past concerts mingled with the excitement of what was to come.

The stage was adorned with vibrant lights that pulsed in sync with the heartbeat of the audience. As the band members took their positions, the roar of the crowd was deafening, a testament to the loyalty and passion of their fanbase. This was not merely a farewell; it was a reunion of souls who had traveled together through the highs and lows of life, united by the universal language of music.

The opening notes of their hit single reverberated through the arena, instantly transporting fans back to the moments that had defined their connection with *Neon Frequencies*. Each chord struck a nostalgic chord, reminding everyone present of the countless road trips, late-night dance parties, and emotional milestones that had been soundtracked by the band's music. It was a collective experience, a shared history that bound them together in a tapestry of sound and emotion.

Dabin, the heart and soul of the band, stood at the forefront, her voice soaring above the crowd, filled with raw emotion. The lyrics resonated deeply, encapsulating the essence of their journey. As she sang, the audience joined in, a powerful chorus of voices harmonizing in tribute to the band that had given them so much. This moment was a vivid reminder of the power of music to evoke memories and emotions, to bring people together in a way that few other experiences could.

The setlist was a carefully curated journey through their discography, each song chosen to evoke specific memories and emotions. From the early hits that had catapulted them to fame to the deeper cuts that showcased their artistic evolution, every note was a reminder of the band's growth and the personal growth of each fan who had followed their journey. As they played, the emotional weight of the moment became palpable; it was a bittersweet celebration of what had been and what was yet to come.

Midway through the concert, the band took a moment to reflect on their journey. Dabin shared heartfelt stories of their early days, the struggles they faced, and the triumphs that followed. She spoke about the fans who had supported them through thick and thin, the friendships forged, and the lessons learned along the way. This moment of vulnerability created a deeper connection between the band and the audience, reminding everyone that they were not just spectators but integral parts of the journey.

As the concert progressed, the energy in the arena reached a crescendo. The band performed their anthems, songs that had become the soundtrack to their fans' lives. Each performance was met with thunderous applause, cheers, and even tears, as the reality of the farewell sank in. The last concert was not just an end; it was a celebration of a legacy that would continue to resonate long after the final note was played.

The final song of the night was a poignant ballad, a fitting tribute to their journey together. As the last notes faded into silence, the audience erupted into a standing ovation, a testament to the impact *Neon Frequencies* had made on their lives. The band members embraced on stage, tears of joy and gratitude streaming down their faces. It was a moment of pure, unfiltered emotion that would be etched in the memory of everyone present.

In conclusion, the last concert of *Neon Frequencies* was a night of nostalgia and celebration, a powerful reminder of the bond forged through music. It encapsulated the essence of their journey, the highs and lows, the laughter and tears, and the unwavering support of their fans. As the lights dimmed for the final time, it was clear that while the band may have played their last note, their legacy would live on in the hearts of those who had been touched by their music. The concert was not just an ending; it was a beautiful beginning of memories that would echo through time.

Life After Neon Frequencies

Dabin's Solo Pursuits: A New Musical Chapter

As the final notes of Neon Frequencies echoed through the arena, Dabin found herself standing at a pivotal crossroads in her musical journey. The end of a band often marks the beginning of a new chapter, and for Dabin, this was no exception. With a heart full of memories and a mind brimming with fresh ideas, she set out to explore her solo pursuits, eager to carve a unique path that would showcase her individuality as an artist.

The Decision to Go Solo

The decision to embark on a solo career was not made lightly. Dabin had spent years harmonizing with her bandmates, creating a sound that resonated with thousands. However, the desire to express her personal artistic vision grew stronger with each passing day. This internal conflict can be likened to the equation of a harmonic oscillator:

$$F = -kx \qquad (73)$$

Where F represents the force of her musical ambitions, k symbolizes the strength of her connection to the band, and x is the distance from her original path. As she leaned further into her individual aspirations, the force of her creative drive intensified, compelling her to break free and explore new soundscapes.

Exploring New Genres

Dabin's solo work began with a deep dive into various musical genres. She experimented with electronic, acoustic, and even orchestral elements, seeking to blend them into a cohesive sound that reflected her growth. This genre-blending approach is reminiscent of the concept of superposition in physics, where multiple states combine to form a new state. In music, this can be represented as:

$$Y(t) = A_1 \sin(\omega_1 t + \phi_1) + A_2 \sin(\omega_2 t + \phi_2) \qquad (74)$$

Where $Y(t)$ represents the resultant sound wave, A_1 and A_2 are the amplitudes of the individual waves, ω denotes their frequencies, and ϕ represents their phase shifts. Dabin skillfully manipulated these elements, creating a sound that was both familiar and refreshingly new.

Collaborations with Diverse Artists

In her quest for artistic authenticity, Dabin sought collaborations with artists from various backgrounds. This not only enriched her sound but also allowed her to share her musical journey with a broader audience. Collaborations can be likened to the concept of synergy, where the whole is greater than the sum of its parts:

$$S = A + B + C + \ldots + n \qquad (75)$$

Where S represents the synergy created, and A, B, C, etc., are the individual contributions of each artist. Dabin's collaborations resulted in tracks that resonated deeply with listeners, as each artist brought their unique flavor to the mix.

The Creative Process: Writing and Recording

The creative process for Dabin's solo album was both exhilarating and daunting. She found herself writing songs that were deeply personal, reflecting her experiences, emotions, and the lessons learned throughout her career. The process can be broken down into several stages:

- **Inspiration:** Drawing from her life experiences, Dabin penned lyrics that resonated with authenticity.
- **Composition:** She composed melodies that complemented her lyrics, often experimenting with unconventional chord progressions.
- **Recording:** The studio became her sanctuary, where she could refine her sound, layer tracks, and experiment with production techniques.

A notable challenge during the recording process was maintaining the balance between her artistic vision and the technical aspects of music production. This balance can be represented mathematically as:

$$P = \frac{A}{T} \tag{76}$$

Where P is the product of her artistic expression, A is her creative output, and T is the time invested in technical refinement. Dabin learned that while creativity is essential, the technical side of music cannot be overlooked.

The Release and Reception of Her Solo Album

Upon the release of her debut solo album, Dabin felt a mixture of excitement and trepidation. The reception from fans and critics alike was overwhelmingly positive, validating her decision to pursue a solo career. The album's success can be analyzed through the lens of the diffusion of innovation theory, which posits that new ideas and products spread through specific channels over time:

$$I(t) = M(1 - e^{-\beta t}) \tag{77}$$

Where $I(t)$ represents the cumulative adoption of her music over time, M is the maximum potential audience, β is the rate of adoption, and t is time. Dabin's

The Impact of Social Media

With the rise of social media platforms, each member utilized these tools to connect with their audience in unprecedented ways. Dabin, Alex, Jamie, and Mark shared their creative processes, personal stories, and behind-the-scenes glimpses into their lives, fostering a sense of intimacy with their fans.

$$\text{Engagement} = (\text{Content Quality}) \times (\text{Frequency of Posts}) \qquad (82)$$

This equation illustrates that the level of engagement each member achieved was directly related to the quality of the content they shared and how often they interacted with their audience.

Legacy and Future Endeavors

As the members of Neon Frequencies ventured into their solo careers, they not only sought to establish their identities but also aimed to honor the legacy of the band. Collaborations among them continued, with occasional guest appearances at each other's shows, reminding fans of the magic they once created together.

The future holds endless possibilities for Dabin and her bandmates. Whether through solo albums, collaborative projects, or ventures into other artistic fields, their journeys are a testament to their resilience and creativity.

In conclusion, the transition from a band to solo careers is fraught with challenges but also filled with opportunities for growth and self-discovery. The members of Neon Frequencies exemplify this journey, proving that while the band may have ended, their musical stories are far from over.

The Extended Legacy: Fans and Future Impact

The legacy of Neon Frequencies extends far beyond the final notes played on their farewell tour. It is woven into the fabric of their devoted fanbase and resonates through the music industry as a whole. This section explores the multifaceted impact the band has had on its fans and the future of music, highlighting the enduring connections forged through their artistry.

The Devoted Fanbase

Neon Frequencies cultivated a passionate and diverse fanbase, characterized by their unwavering support and dedication. Fans were not merely passive listeners; they were active participants in the band's journey. The phenomenon of fandom can be understood through the lens of social identity theory, which posits that individuals derive a sense of self from their group affiliations. For many, being a part of the Neon Frequencies community provided a sense of belonging and identity.

The band's concerts transformed into communal experiences, where fans united to celebrate their shared love for the music. The emotional connection fostered during live performances created a powerful bond between the band and their audience, often leading to lifelong loyalty. This phenomenon is exemplified in the case of the "Neon Hearts," a dedicated fan group that organized meet-ups, charity events, and social media campaigns to promote the band's music and values.

Influencing Future Generations

The influence of Neon Frequencies on future musicians cannot be overstated. Their innovative sound and genre-blending approach inspired countless aspiring artists to experiment with their musical identities. This is particularly evident in the rise of new artists who cite Dabin and the band as pivotal influences in their creative journeys.

For instance, consider the case of emerging artist Lira Voss, whose debut album incorporates elements of electronic, rock, and orchestral music—a testament to the diverse sonic palette that Neon Frequencies championed. Lira has openly expressed her admiration for Dabin's ability to fuse genres seamlessly, stating, "Neon Frequencies taught me that music knows no boundaries. It's about expressing yourself, no matter the style."

Philanthropic Endeavors and Social Impact

Beyond music, the band utilized their platform to effect positive change in the world. Through various philanthropic endeavors, Neon Frequencies demonstrated a commitment to social responsibility. Dabin's involvement in charitable initiatives, such as music education programs for underprivileged youth, exemplifies the band's dedication to giving back to the community.

The impact of these efforts can be quantified through the concept of social capital, which refers to the networks of relationships among people that enable society to function effectively. By leveraging their fame for good, Neon Frequencies not only enhanced their legacy but also fostered a sense of community and empowerment among their fans.

For example, the "Music for Change" campaign, initiated by the band, raised over $1 million for various causes, including mental health awareness and environmental conservation. This initiative galvanized fans to participate, proving that music can be a catalyst for social change.

Legacy in Popular Culture

The cultural footprint of Neon Frequencies continues to thrive in popular culture. Their music has been featured in films, television shows, and advertisements, ensuring that their sound remains relevant in contemporary media. The integration of their songs into various forms of entertainment serves as a testament to the band's universal appeal and the timelessness of their artistry.

Moreover, the band's aesthetic and imagery have inspired fashion trends and visual art, further solidifying their place in the cultural zeitgeist. The iconic neon colors and vibrant visuals associated with Neon Frequencies have been adopted by fans and artists alike, creating a distinct visual language that resonates with the band's ethos.

Conclusion

In conclusion, the extended legacy of Neon Frequencies is a rich tapestry woven from the threads of their devoted fanbase, their influence on future generations of musicians, their philanthropic efforts, and their enduring presence in popular culture. As fans continue to celebrate their music and values, the impact of Neon Frequencies will be felt for years to come. Their journey serves as a reminder of the power of music to unite, inspire, and create lasting change in the world.

Neon Frequencies: The Reunion?

Reunion Rumors and Speculations: Hope for an Encore

The world of music is rife with stories of reunions, each filled with anticipation, nostalgia, and a hint of skepticism. For the devoted fans of Neon Frequencies, whispers of a reunion have sparked a flurry of excitement and speculation. This section delves into the dynamics of these rumors, exploring the underlying theories, potential challenges, and the fervent hopes of fans yearning for an encore.

The Genesis of Reunion Rumors

Reunion rumors often emerge from a variety of sources, including social media interactions, public appearances, and interviews. In the case of Neon Frequencies, the initial spark ignited when band members began sharing nostalgic posts on their social media platforms, reminiscing about their journey together. These posts, often accompanied by behind-the-scenes footage and old photographs, reignited the flames of speculation among fans.

Theories surrounding reunions can be analyzed through the lens of social psychology, particularly the concept of *collective nostalgia*. According to [?], collective nostalgia refers to a shared longing for the past that strengthens group identity. In the context of Neon Frequencies, fans collectively reminisce about the band's heyday, creating a powerful emotional bond that fuels desires for a reunion.

Challenges in the Reunion Process

While the allure of a reunion is undeniable, the path to rekindling the magic of Neon Frequencies is fraught with challenges. One of the primary obstacles is the *creative differences* that may have led to the band's initial disbandment. As artists evolve, their musical directions may diverge significantly, complicating the potential for collaborative efforts.

Mathematically, we can represent the dynamics of band member compatibility as a function of time and individual creative trajectories. Let $C(t)$ denote the compatibility factor over time t, which can be expressed as:

$$C(t) = \frac{A(t) \cdot B(t)}{D(t)}$$

where $A(t)$ and $B(t)$ are the creative outputs of the individual members, and $D(t)$ represents the distance between their artistic visions. As t increases, the divergence in musical styles may lead to a decrease in $C(t)$, thereby complicating reunion efforts.

Examples of Successful Reunions

Despite these challenges, history is replete with examples of successful reunions that have captured the hearts of fans. Bands like Fleetwood Mac and The Eagles have demonstrated that with the right combination of nostalgia, mutual respect, and a shared vision, the magic can be reignited. The key lies in the willingness of the members to set aside past grievances and focus on their collective passion for music.

For instance, Fleetwood Mac's reunion for the *The Dance* tour in 1997 was marked by a renewed sense of camaraderie and artistic collaboration. The band members acknowledged their differences but emphasized the importance of their shared history and the joy of performing together. This approach not only revitalized their careers but also deepened their connection with fans.

Reflecting on Challenges and Triumphs

As they reconnected, the bandmates also confronted the challenges they had faced during their time apart—creative differences, personal struggles, and the pressures of fame. They engaged in candid conversations about their experiences, acknowledging how these challenges had shaped them both individually and collectively.

The process of reflection was cathartic, allowing them to heal old wounds and strengthen their bond. It became clear that the trials they had faced were not just obstacles but integral parts of their journey that had contributed to their growth as artists.

The Vision for the Future

With rekindled connections and a renewed sense of purpose, the bandmates began to envision the future of Neon Frequencies. They discussed the possibility of a reunion tour, one that would celebrate their legacy while introducing a new generation of fans to their music.

This vision was not merely about nostalgia; it was about evolution. They aimed to create a new album that would encapsulate their journey, blending the sounds of their past with the influences they had embraced during their time apart. The prospect of collaborating again filled them with excitement and determination.

Conclusion: A New Chapter

In reconnecting and reflecting, the members of Neon Frequencies discovered that the magic of their collaboration was not lost but merely transformed. They emerged from their reunion not only as bandmates but as lifelong friends, united by their shared passion for music and the experiences that had shaped them.

The rekindling of their creative flame paved the way for a new chapter in their musical journey—one that promised to honor their roots while exploring uncharted territories. As they prepared to step back into the spotlight, the anticipation of what lay ahead filled the air, igniting a sense of hope and excitement for the future of Neon Frequencies.

The Reunion Tour: A Second Chance to Relive the Glory

After years of speculation and whispers among fans, the moment arrived when Neon Frequencies announced their reunion tour. It was a decision that sent ripples of excitement through the music community, reigniting the flames of nostalgia that had long been simmering in the hearts of their devoted followers. The tour was not merely a series of concerts; it was a celebration of the legacy that the band had built over the years, offering both old and new fans a chance to relive the magic that had made them a phenomenon.

The Build-Up to the Reunion

In the months leading up to the announcement, social media buzzed with rumors. Fans shared their favorite memories of concerts past, and hashtags like #NeonFrequenciesReunion began trending. The band members, now seasoned artists with their own solo careers, found themselves reflecting on their journey together. Dabin, the creative force behind the group, expressed a longing for the camaraderie and energy that had defined their early days.

The decision to reunite was not without its challenges. Each member had carved out a distinct identity in the years since their last performance. Balancing their individual artistic visions with the collective identity of Neon Frequencies required careful negotiation. The chemistry that once sparked their creativity had to be rekindled, and this process involved revisiting their shared history, discussing their growth, and ultimately finding common ground.

Rehearsals: Rebuilding the Band Dynamic

The reunion rehearsals were a blend of excitement and trepidation. The band members gathered in a studio that felt both familiar and foreign. The first few sessions were marked by laughter and nostalgia, but also by the inevitable tension that arises when old friends reunite after a long separation. Each member brought their unique experiences and influences to the table, and while this enriched their sound, it also sparked creative disagreements.

To navigate these challenges, the band adopted a collaborative approach. They revisited classic hits while also experimenting with new material. This process mirrored the mathematical principle of *synergy*, where the whole becomes greater than the sum of its parts. The equation can be represented as:

$$S = \sum_{i=1}^{n} x_i + \sum_{j=1}^{m} y_j \tag{85}$$

Where S is the synergy created, x_i represents the contributions of individual members, and y_j reflects the collaborative efforts. This synergy was evident as they crafted a setlist that balanced fan favorites with fresh tracks, showcasing their evolution as artists.

The Tour Experience: A Rollercoaster of Emotions

As the tour kicked off, the atmosphere was electric. Fans from different generations filled the venues, creating a vibrant tapestry of excitement and anticipation. The opening night was a testament to the band's enduring appeal, with a sold-out crowd singing along to every lyric.

However, the tour was not without its hurdles. The physical demands of performing night after night took a toll, and the pressures of being in the spotlight reignited old insecurities and conflicts. The band had to navigate the complexities of fame once more, balancing their artistic integrity with the expectations of their audience.

A New Chapter: Merging Old and New

Throughout the tour, Neon Frequencies embraced the idea of merging their classic sound with contemporary influences. The introduction of new technology in their performances—such as augmented reality visuals and interactive elements—created a dynamic experience that resonated with both loyal fans and newcomers. This innovative approach not only revitalized their music but also highlighted their adaptability in a rapidly changing industry.

The reunion tour culminated in a breathtaking finale, where the band performed a medley of their greatest hits intertwined with new material. This blending of past and present was emblematic of their journey, demonstrating that while they had grown and evolved, the essence of Neon Frequencies remained intact.

Legacy and Reflections

As the final notes echoed through the venue, the band took a moment to reflect on their journey. The reunion tour had not only rekindled their bond but also reaffirmed their impact on the music scene. They had created a space where fans could celebrate their shared love for music, and in doing so, they had solidified their legacy.

The tour served as a reminder that while the band may have faced challenges, their commitment to each other and their craft had triumphed. As they took their final bow, the audience erupted in applause, a testament to the enduring power of music to connect people across time and space.

In conclusion, the reunion tour of Neon Frequencies was more than just a nostalgic return; it was a reaffirmation of their artistry, a celebration of their evolution, and a heartfelt connection with their fans. The journey may have been fraught with challenges, but the love for music and the bond between the band members shone brightly, illuminating the path forward as they embraced the next chapter of their musical legacy.

The End of an Era

The Lasting Impact of Neon Frequencies: Immortalized in Music

The journey of Neon Frequencies, from their humble beginnings to their monumental rise in the music industry, has left an indelible mark on the landscape of contemporary music. Their unique sound, characterized by a fusion of genres and innovative production techniques, has not only captivated audiences worldwide but has also influenced a generation of musicians and composers. This section explores the lasting impact of Neon Frequencies, examining their contributions to music theory, cultural significance, and the legacy they leave behind.

Innovative Sound and Musical Techniques

At the core of Neon Frequencies' impact lies their distinctive sound, which seamlessly blends elements from various genres, including electronic, rock, pop, and indie. This genre-blending approach can be understood through the lens of music theory, particularly the concept of *polystylism*, where multiple styles coexist within a single piece. The band's ability to incorporate complex rhythms, unconventional time signatures, and rich harmonic progressions has set a new standard for creativity in music production.

For instance, their hit single "Electric Dreams" employs a *7/8 time signature*, a rarity in mainstream music, which creates an engaging and unpredictable listening experience. The use of this time signature can be mathematically expressed as:

$$\text{Total Beats} = 7 \quad \text{(in a measure)} \tag{86}$$

This rhythmic complexity not only showcases their technical prowess but also invites listeners to engage more deeply with the music, challenging traditional notions of pop structure.

Cultural Significance and Influence

Neon Frequencies have transcended the realm of mere entertainment; they have become cultural icons. Their music resonates with themes of self-discovery, love, and societal change, reflecting the struggles and aspirations of their generation.

but also for the stories behind each piece, showcasing how deeply the band's music resonated with their audience.

Community Gatherings and Events

As the farewell tour approached, fan communities organized meet-ups to celebrate the band's legacy. From small gatherings in local cafes to larger events in parks, fans shared their favorite memories, played *Neon Frequencies* tracks, and even held karaoke nights. These communal experiences fostered a sense of unity among fans, reinforcing the idea that the music had created a family-like atmosphere. One such gathering in Los Angeles drew over a hundred fans, who collectively sang their favorite songs, creating an impromptu concert that echoed the band's spirit.

Memorializing the Band's Impact

In the wake of the farewell tour, fans initiated several tribute projects aimed at immortalizing the band's contributions to music. One significant initiative was the creation of a documentary titled "Neon Frequencies: The Soundtrack of Our Lives." This film featured interviews with fans, industry professionals, and even the band members, reflecting on the journey and the impact of their music. The documentary served as a powerful reminder of the band's legacy, showcasing how their sound transcended mere entertainment to become a vital part of fans' identities.

Fan Rituals and Merchandise

As a testament to their loyalty, fans also engaged in various rituals to honor *Neon Frequencies*. Many adorned themselves with tattoos of lyrics or symbols associated with the band, creating a permanent tribute to their love for the music. Additionally, limited-edition merchandise, such as vinyl records and commemorative t-shirts, sold out within hours, illustrating the fervor and commitment of the fanbase. The phrase "Forever Neon" became a rallying cry, encapsulating the enduring spirit of the band within the hearts of their fans.

Legacy of Love and Inspiration

The reactions and tributes from fans encapsulated the essence of what *Neon Frequencies* represented: a beacon of hope, love, and inspiration. The band's music had a unique ability to connect with listeners on a profound level, addressing themes of love, loss, and the pursuit of dreams. As the final notes of their last concert echoed into the night, fans left not only with memories of the music but with a renewed sense of belonging and understanding of their own journeys.

In conclusion, the farewell of *Neon Frequencies* was not merely the end of a musical chapter but the beginning of a legacy that would continue to inspire future generations. The emotional tributes, creative expressions, and community bonds forged during this time serve as a testament to the indelible mark the band left on the world of music and the hearts of their fans. As they look back on this extraordinary journey, fans will forever carry the spirit of *Neon Frequencies* within them, reminding us all that music is not just heard, but felt, lived, and cherished.

Saying Goodbye to Neon Frequencies: A Final Farewell

As the final notes of Neon Frequencies echoed through the stadium, a palpable wave of emotion swept over the crowd. This was not just another concert; it was a culmination of years of passion, creativity, and connection. The band had become more than just a musical entity; they had evolved into a cultural phenomenon, resonating deeply with fans across the globe. This farewell was a bittersweet moment, a poignant reminder of the journey they had taken together.

The atmosphere was electric, charged with anticipation and nostalgia. Fans, many of whom had followed Neon Frequencies from their humble beginnings, gathered to witness the end of an era. The setlist was a carefully curated blend of their greatest hits, each song a chapter in the story of their rise to fame. As the lights dimmed and the first chords rang out, a collective cheer erupted, a testament to the bond forged between the band and their fans.

The emotional weight of the farewell tour was underscored by the heartfelt speeches delivered by band members throughout the evening. Dabin, the driving force behind the group, took a moment to reflect on the journey they had shared. "This isn't just a goodbye," she said, her voice trembling with emotion. "It's a celebration of everything we've accomplished together. Each of you has been a part of our story, and we will carry you with us in our hearts."

In the moments that followed, the band performed their iconic anthem, *"Neon Dreams,"* a song that encapsulated their ethos. The lyrics spoke of hope, perseverance, and the transformative power of music. As the chorus rang out, fans sang along, their voices melding into a powerful choir that reverberated throughout the venue. This shared experience highlighted the unique relationship between the band and their audience, a connection that transcended mere entertainment.

The final act of the concert was a medley of emotional ballads, showcasing the depth of Dabin's songwriting and the band's musical evolution. Each note struck a chord within the audience, as memories flooded back—first concerts, late-night jam sessions, and the thrill of discovering new music together. It was a moment of collective reflection, where the past and present converged in a beautiful tapestry of sound.

As the last song concluded, the band members embraced on stage, tears glistening in their eyes. They took a moment to soak in the applause, the cheers, and the love emanating from the audience. It was a moment of closure, a final farewell that resonated with everyone present. The lights dimmed, and the crowd erupted into a standing ovation, a tribute to the indelible mark Neon Frequencies had left on their lives.

In the days that followed, social media was flooded with tributes from fans expressing their gratitude and love for the band. Hashtags like #FarewellNeonFrequencies and #ForeverInOurHearts trended worldwide, as fans shared their favorite memories, concert photos, and personal stories. This outpouring of affection served as a reminder that while the band may have disbanded, their music would continue to live on in the hearts of those who had been touched by it.

The legacy of Neon Frequencies was not just in their chart-topping hits or sold-out shows; it was in the community they had fostered. Fans had formed friendships, found solace in the music, and created a culture of support and love. Dabin's philanthropic efforts, inspired by her journey, would further solidify the band's impact on the world, as she continued to advocate for mental health awareness and music education.

In conclusion, the farewell of Neon Frequencies marked the end of a remarkable chapter in music history. Their journey was one of growth, creativity, and connection, leaving behind a legacy that would inspire future generations of musicians and fans alike. As the final curtain fell, it was clear that while Neon Frequencies may have said goodbye, their spirit would forever resonate in the hearts of those who had experienced the magic of their music. The final farewell was not an end, but a celebration of a journey that would continue to inspire long after the last note had faded.

Index

-doubt, 107

a, 1–28, 30, 32–34, 36–42, 44–49, 51–57, 61–70, 72–87, 89–101, 103–129, 131, 132, 134–145, 147–162, 164–177, 179, 180
ability, 2, 3, 5, 8–10, 12–14, 27, 35, 39, 41, 54, 56, 57, 69, 79, 81, 82, 88, 94, 100, 108, 110, 112, 117, 123, 124, 130, 136, 143, 151, 159, 165, 170, 177
abundance, 94
acceptance, 103
accident, 66
acclaim, 111
acknowledgment, 4, 148, 157
acoustic, 79, 109, 110, 112, 136, 150, 157
act, 38, 55, 85, 90, 94, 119, 148, 151, 157
adaptability, 19, 41, 56, 73, 111, 150, 152
addiction, 92, 101, 103
addition, 65, 86
admiration, 4, 23, 89, 91
adoration, 92, 129

adrenaline, 62, 63, 65, 94, 97
advance, 85
advancement, 54
advent, 54
adventure, 61, 63, 65, 67
adversity, 69, 158, 159
advertising, 49
advocate, 103, 145
aesthetic, 80, 168
affiliation, 82
affinity, 13
age, 1–3, 8–13, 51, 82, 87, 138
agency, 83
air, 1, 4, 8, 15, 23, 63, 120, 148, 159, 160
airplay, 52–54
album, 27, 41, 45–47, 73, 86, 100, 110, 111, 118–120, 122–125, 128, 144, 147, 149–151, 153, 155, 172
alcohol, 92, 95
Alex, 23, 24, 165, 166
Alex Chen, 126
alignment, 25, 35
alliance, 23
allure, 92, 93, 95, 114, 170
amalgamation, 118
ambiance, 70

181

chase, 62
check, 155
cheer, 179
chemistry, 24–28, 33, 44, 48, 66, 99, 144, 151, 164, 171, 173
chess, 67
child, 1, 3, 8, 10
childhood, 2, 4–6, 8, 10, 11, 16, 18
chord, 5, 14, 15
choreography, 81
chorus, 78, 160
city, 65, 66, 122, 158
clarity, 121
clash, 120
class, 15
classification, 112, 113
climax, 62
clock, 54
closure, 148, 155, 180
cloud, 32
co, 27, 110
coffee, 19, 23, 66, 70
coherence, 18
cohesion, 76, 100
coincidence, 25
collaboration, 12, 16, 22, 24–26, 30–35, 38, 47, 62, 63, 68–70, 104, 109–111, 115, 116, 119, 126, 128, 134, 135, 137, 140, 144, 145, 147, 148, 155, 164, 170, 172
collaborator, 165
collection, 122
collective, 17, 31, 33, 35, 61, 91, 125, 126, 144, 147–149, 151, 155, 158, 164, 169, 170, 173, 179

combination, 3, 9, 10, 25, 56, 123, 169
comfort, 40
commitment, 38, 44, 56, 57, 73, 82, 83, 87, 90, 104, 110, 116, 137, 138, 141–143, 152, 165, 167, 174
communication, 16, 27, 51, 62, 65, 69, 86, 100, 101, 144, 155
community, 33, 44, 47–49, 55, 82–84, 86, 87, 89–91, 98, 103, 126, 138, 144, 145, 151, 152, 155, 159, 167, 172, 176
companion, 11, 66
complexity, 5, 9, 83, 112, 118, 175
component, 14, 65
composition, 10–12, 15, 134
compromise, 16, 62, 144
concept, 9, 15, 27, 68, 111, 117, 127, 162, 167
concert, 44, 62, 63, 73, 77–79, 81, 85, 90, 95, 104, 105, 148, 151, 157, 159, 161, 179
conclusion, 6, 8, 33, 38, 40, 44, 47, 49, 51, 54, 57, 67, 69, 74, 81, 84, 89, 94, 98, 100, 103, 105, 108, 111, 113, 116, 117, 120, 122, 124, 129, 136, 138, 140, 143, 145, 148, 151, 153, 155, 158, 160, 164, 166, 168, 174, 177, 180
condition, 62
confidence, 10, 12, 16
conflict, 26, 34, 67–70, 84, 85, 93, 99–101, 128, 162
connection, 9, 10, 12, 14, 17, 22, 23, 26, 27, 44, 48, 62, 77,

Index   185

79–85, 87, 89, 98, 105,
106, 116, 120, 124, 140,
143, 144, 151, 152, 161,
165, 167, 174, 176, 179,
180
connectivity, 134, 138
constant, 11, 20, 66, 86, 88, 96, 108, 129
construct, 14
constructivism, 126
contemporary, 7, 10, 13, 15, 20, 110, 112, 113, 116, 120, 136, 168, 175
content, 14, 22, 54, 87, 88, 138, 149, 154, 166
contrast, 112
control, 92
copyright, 133
core, 19, 39, 69, 74, 84
cornerstone, 16, 20, 38, 44, 49, 52, 63, 89, 143, 144
cost, 93, 108
country, 133
course, 23
coverage, 52
craft, 3, 11, 17, 44, 54, 72, 80, 96, 117, 140, 174
crash, 101
creation, 15, 21, 46, 63, 68, 70, 75, 83, 100, 136, 151
creativity, 2, 4, 6, 8, 10, 12, 13, 16–18, 22, 24, 26, 27, 30, 36, 38, 40–42, 45–47, 54, 63, 69, 70, 83, 91, 94, 96, 98, 105, 106, 111, 116, 117, 124, 126, 130, 136, 140, 144, 148, 154, 155, 165, 166, 173, 179, 180
crescendo, 70, 161

crew, 97
crisis, 62
criticism, 12, 152
cross, 135–137
crowd, 4, 23, 77–79, 85, 94, 160, 174, 179, 180
crucible, 30, 42, 47, 70
crystallization, 164
cuisine, 66
culmination, 3, 32, 81, 122, 155, 159, 179
cultivation, 139, 140
culture, 66, 67, 83, 89, 91–93, 95, 101, 103, 142, 143, 168
curiosity, 10
curriculum, 15
curse, 7
curtain, 158, 164, 180
cycle, 93, 98, 107

Dabin, 1–27, 30, 33, 39–42, 44, 46, 63–65, 68, 70, 78, 79, 84–87, 92, 93, 97, 98, 100, 101, 103, 104, 106–120, 124, 126, 129–131, 135, 136, 139–145, 149, 152, 160–162, 164–167, 171
dance, 20, 25
data, 133
date, 130
David Bowie, 1
day, 1, 9, 25, 63, 162
deadline, 41
debt, 93
debut, 27, 41, 45, 47, 73, 122, 124
decade, 54, 57
decision, 66, 100, 124, 148, 162, 172, 173
declaration, 3

decline, 98
dedication, 3, 8, 17, 38, 44, 54, 90, 96, 105, 159, 166, 167
definition, 156
delivery, 5, 14
demand, 156
departure, 113, 125, 127
dependency, 101
depression, 93
depth, 3, 15, 21, 22, 98, 111, 116, 117, 122, 125, 128, 149, 156, 171, 176
design, 72–74, 80, 104
desire, 10, 12, 39, 45, 84, 93, 109, 111, 112, 118, 125, 152, 162
destination, 108
destiny, 25
determination, 2, 45, 172
development, 4, 14–16, 25, 28, 101, 152
devotion, 83, 84, 91
dexterity, 8
dialogue, 91, 100, 135, 136
dichotomy, 126
difference, 143
dilemma, 39, 119
dilution, 18
dim, 63
direction, 26, 49, 68, 73, 84, 107, 111, 118–120, 124, 126, 128, 149, 152
disagreement, 26, 100
disappointment, 86
discipline, 11, 13
discography, 112, 160
discomfort, 67
discord, 67, 70, 101, 152
discovery, 166, 175

discussion, 93, 100
dissatisfaction, 86
dissemination, 83, 87
distance, 13
distress, 98
distribution, 133
diversity, 100, 129, 136, 138, 165
doubt, 107
down, 36, 70, 155
drive, 66
driving, 28, 33, 66, 84
drummer, 23, 68, 70, 128
drumming, 24
duality, 67, 129
dynamic, 5, 22, 24, 25, 27, 28, 51, 67, 73, 76, 80, 99, 100, 112, 118, 119, 150

ease, 3
echo, 61, 141
ecosystem, 81
edge, 156
edition, 90
education, 11, 14, 16, 167
effect, 48, 51, 142, 167
effectiveness, 86, 132, 142
effort, 95, 111, 118, 122, 144
element, 47, 73, 91
embrace, 17, 22, 32, 108, 148, 155, 164, 170
emergence, 4
emotion, 2, 8, 9, 44, 79, 84, 112, 128, 147, 148, 155, 158, 160, 179
empowerment, 167
encore, 168, 170
encounter, 23
encouragement, 79

Index   187

end, 25, 61, 116, 148, 160, 161, 179, 180
endeavor, 31, 36, 52, 79, 136, 149
ending, 160
energy, 4, 8, 11, 18, 24, 27, 41, 42, 47, 48, 63, 65–68, 76, 78–80, 82, 84, 95, 104, 148, 159, 161, 165
engagement, 12, 55, 76, 78, 80, 84–88, 91, 123, 133, 159, 166, 176
engineer, 47, 121
engineering, 80, 104
entertainment, 48, 141, 168, 175
enthusiasm, 79, 104
entity, 179
entry, 133
environment, 1, 2, 7, 8, 10–12, 26, 34, 37, 63, 70, 79, 97, 100, 117, 128, 131, 144, 154, 155
equation, 4, 8, 13, 19–21, 29, 30, 35, 46, 47, 52, 55, 56, 58, 72, 90, 97, 100, 107, 112, 117–119, 125, 127, 128, 134, 136–138, 158, 159, 162, 164–166
equilibrium, 129
equipment, 41, 62, 64, 67, 73, 79, 81
era, 57, 120, 148, 179
essence, 1, 2, 4, 5, 10, 13, 27, 28, 42, 44, 47, 74, 91, 109, 122, 147, 150, 158–160, 171, 174
establishment, 83
ethic, 17
ethos, 91, 168
euphoria, 103, 151
evening, 23

event, 16, 23, 74, 81, 85, 86
evidence, 7
evolution, 20, 22, 23, 38, 54, 67, 79–81, 83, 84, 99, 109, 111, 116, 118, 120, 124, 126, 128, 129, 135, 150–152, 156, 160, 172, 174
example, 7, 27, 41, 44, 46, 64, 68, 79, 85, 90, 109–111, 117, 127, 128, 137, 150
exception, 92, 161
excess, 92–95
exchange, 49, 84, 134, 136–138, 150
excitement, 15, 26, 38, 54, 61–65, 73, 84, 86, 94, 96, 156, 168, 172–174
exclusivity, 85
execution, 74
exhaustion, 17, 152
exhilaration, 63, 101
experience, 12, 13, 16, 17, 25, 30, 40, 41, 44, 55, 63, 66, 67, 72, 73, 77, 79, 80, 84–86, 91, 94, 98, 103, 111–113, 120, 124, 126, 131, 144, 145, 151, 153, 156, 159, 176
experiment, 10, 13, 21, 32, 48, 61, 63, 79, 109, 125, 127, 136, 152, 167
experimentation, 21, 22, 38–40, 42, 126, 127, 150, 151, 171
exploration, 6, 8, 10, 11, 18–20, 22, 79, 109, 112, 113, 115, 118, 126, 152, 155, 164
explosion, 55
exposure, 20, 52–54
expression, 2, 10, 11, 17, 33, 36, 89, 101, 109, 120, 124, 126,

homesickness, 64
hometown, 65
hope, 82, 143, 150, 170
horizon, 89
hotel, 62, 66
house, 113
household, 8, 20, 23
humanity, 136
hurdle, 41, 133
hybridity, 127
hype, 47–49

ice, 85
idea, 27, 30, 36, 63, 109, 118, 144, 150, 155
ideal, 97
identification, 82
identity, 2, 5–9, 11–13, 15, 18–20, 23, 25, 28, 30, 39, 45, 47, 61, 63, 65, 67, 69, 74, 79, 81, 82, 89, 90, 109, 111, 114, 116, 118, 119, 136, 143, 144, 147, 152, 153, 166, 167, 171, 173
image, 93, 95, 129
imagery, 168
imagination, 1, 11, 13
impact, 4, 5, 26, 33, 51, 52, 54, 64, 84, 85, 88, 91, 98, 103, 115–117, 122, 126, 135, 137, 138, 143, 148, 151, 159, 164, 166–168, 174, 175, 177
importance, 8, 13, 41, 66, 67, 69, 98, 111, 116, 119, 126, 135, 138, 144, 145, 152, 159
impression, 27
improvement, 121

in, 1–28, 30, 32–35, 40–42, 44, 45, 47–49, 51–57, 61–63, 65–67, 69, 70, 72–74, 77, 79–87, 89–96, 98, 100, 101, 103, 104, 106–114, 116–129, 131–145, 147–152, 154, 155, 157–161, 164–175, 177, 179, 180
inception, 116, 149
incident, 41, 66, 158
inclusion, 127
inclusivity, 138
incorporation, 19, 123, 128, 136
indie, 110, 112
individual, 7, 26, 28, 30, 68, 84, 91, 120, 126, 147, 164, 171, 173
individuality, 124, 162
indulgence, 95
industry, 4, 5, 12, 23, 25, 27, 28, 33, 45, 48, 49, 51, 53, 54, 56, 57, 65, 70, 81, 89, 92–95, 101, 103, 106–109, 111, 116, 118, 120, 122, 126, 129, 138, 141–144, 150, 166, 175
inevitability, 147
influence, 2, 3, 5, 10, 15, 20, 30, 49, 54, 57, 89, 91, 93, 110, 117, 138–141, 167, 168
information, 49
infusion, 3, 126
ingredient, 144
innovation, 16, 20, 22, 26, 34, 38–40, 54, 69, 70, 81, 99, 100, 109, 111, 112, 114, 116, 117, 138, 165, 171
input, 128, 150

Index

inspiration, 3, 6, 33, 36, 70, 109, 111, 112, 119, 125, 138, 143, 149, 154
instance, 5, 15, 20, 25–27, 41, 66, 67, 70, 73, 81, 85, 91, 100, 112, 117, 122, 126, 128, 136, 144, 150, 152
instructor, 9
instrument, 11, 13
instrumentation, 58, 112, 113, 117, 123, 150
integration, 32, 39, 73, 109, 127, 156, 168
integrity, 61, 95, 119, 174
intent, 3
interaction, 44, 77, 79, 83, 85, 86
interactivity, 88
interconnectedness, 126
interest, 2, 11, 106
interplay, 6, 13, 22, 28, 44, 54, 70, 113, 117–119, 122, 126, 136
intersection, 8, 91
intimacy, 157, 166
introduction, 80, 128, 129
introspection, 93, 131
investment, 82
invitation, 120
involvement, 141, 167
isolation, 64, 108, 144
issue, 18, 27, 86

Jackson, 7
jam, 3, 8, 24, 26, 27, 34, 41, 46, 62, 63, 66, 70, 98, 158, 171
Jamie, 165, 166
jazz, 18
Joni Mitchell, 1
journey, 2, 4, 6, 8, 10, 12–15, 17, 20–23, 25, 28, 30, 33, 36, 38, 40, 42, 44, 45, 47, 49, 52, 54, 56, 61, 62, 65, 67, 69, 79, 81–84, 87, 89, 90, 92, 93, 96, 98, 99, 101, 103, 105, 106, 108, 109, 111, 112, 116, 118, 120, 122, 124, 129, 131, 138, 141, 143–145, 147–162, 164, 166, 168, 171, 172, 174, 175, 177, 179, 180
Joy, 158
joy, 11, 62, 84, 93, 94, 107, 152, 171

key, 15, 36, 37, 73, 74, 133, 169
keyboard, 8
knowledge, 17, 126

labor, 95
labyrinth, 51
lack, 18
landmark, 81
landscape, 4, 11, 13, 32, 51, 52, 54, 81, 89, 106, 109, 111, 114, 116, 120, 134, 136, 138–140, 158, 165, 175
language, 1, 9, 83, 160, 168
laughter, 67, 158, 171, 173
layer, 5, 22, 116, 156
layering, 42, 100
layout, 73
lead, 7, 25, 26, 28, 34, 40, 41, 46, 64, 67, 68, 86, 88, 90, 92–97, 112, 121, 125, 129, 134, 136
leadership, 26
leap, 120
learning, 9, 11, 12, 66, 145, 176

leave, 2, 12, 175
legacy, 1, 7, 25, 28, 33, 44, 57, 70, 89–92, 111, 118, 124, 138–140, 143, 145, 150, 151, 153, 158, 159, 161, 166–168, 170, 172–175, 180
lens, 19, 25, 98, 109, 117, 126, 136, 166
lesson, 144
level, 8, 63, 85, 113, 116, 119, 131, 134, 164, 166
levity, 67
life, 2, 3, 10, 11, 17, 23, 42, 44, 61, 63, 65–67, 72, 83, 90, 93, 94, 96–98, 103, 118, 129, 131, 160
lifeblood, 70
lifestyle, 65, 92–96, 107
lifetime, 67
light, 2, 73, 104, 140, 156
lighting, 72–74, 79, 80
Lila, 110
limelight, 52
line, 94, 96, 112
lineage, 7
lineup, 33, 34, 129
linger, 151, 159
listener, 113, 135
listening, 86
live, 12, 26, 27, 42, 44, 56, 62, 63, 65, 74, 77, 79, 81, 89, 94, 113, 122, 123, 144, 151, 167
living, 1, 93
local, 4, 9, 11, 12, 23, 27, 47, 49, 54, 61, 66, 79, 81, 82, 84, 141, 142, 158
location, 32, 85, 158
lodging, 66

loneliness, 97
longevity, 25
longing, 97, 117, 154
look, 159
loop, 53, 56, 79, 141, 142, 150
Los Angeles, 85
loss, 82, 91, 119, 152
love, 2, 13, 17, 82, 91, 96, 98, 119, 160, 167, 174, 175, 180
loyalty, 90, 160, 167
luck, 52
luxury, 92
lyric, 32, 90, 151, 164, 174
lyricist, 149

magic, 10, 33, 37, 63, 70, 72, 77, 160, 166, 169, 170, 172, 173, 180
mainstream, 51, 53, 54
making, 28, 31, 63, 85, 100, 107, 150
management, 85, 93
manifestation, 91
Mark, 165, 166
mark, 2, 4, 12, 18, 25, 33, 57, 117, 118, 136, 139, 153, 164, 175, 180
market, 132, 133
marketability, 143
marketing, 54, 82, 86, 132, 133
Maslow, 98
mastering, 47, 121
masterpiece, 37
material, 174
matrix, 34
matter, 33, 52, 67
maturity, 3
meaning, 98, 119, 126
means, 11, 17, 57, 61, 81, 110, 116

media, 48, 51–54, 56, 82–89, 106, 123, 138, 144, 151, 156, 166–168
meditation, 65
medley, 174
meet, 7, 84–86, 144, 167
meeting, 25, 107
melding, 5
melody, 9, 13, 68, 70, 113, 125
melting, 46, 126
member, 24, 26–28, 32, 41, 46, 62, 65, 67, 69, 70, 72, 79, 100, 111, 120, 144, 147, 148, 150, 155, 164, 166, 171, 173
memorabilia, 89–91
memory, 67, 149, 158, 170
mentor, 14, 145
mentorship, 14
merchandise, 90
metamorphosis, 42
metaphor, 8
method, 30
metric, 132
Mia, 23, 24, 68
mic, 12, 23, 47
mid, 62
middle, 158
midnight, 54
Midway, 161
mind, 161, 171
mindfulness, 130
minimum, 72
minute, 64
misadventure, 67
miscommunication, 66, 73
miss, 66
mission, 45
misstep, 129

Mitchell, 5
mix, 15, 58, 121, 126, 135, 159
mixing, 47, 58, 121
mixture, 4
model, 87, 137, 138, 176
moment, 3, 4, 8, 11, 16, 26, 27, 54, 55, 62, 63, 65–68, 70, 90, 100, 110, 120, 122, 148, 156, 157, 159–161, 172, 174, 179, 180
momentum, 31
mood, 73
morale, 88
motel, 66
mother, 10
mouth, 49–51, 82
move, 67, 123, 128
movement, 177
movie, 62
Mozart, 8
multitude, 75, 112, 113
mundane, 23, 65
music, 1–5, 7–17, 19, 20, 22–28, 30–33, 36, 38, 41, 42, 44–49, 51–57, 62, 63, 65–70, 72–74, 77, 79–84, 86–89, 91–94, 96, 98–101, 103–109, 111–114, 116–118, 120, 122–124, 126–129, 131, 133, 135–145, 148, 149, 151, 152, 154, 155, 158–160, 163–172, 174, 175, 177, 180
musicality, 8
musician, 12, 14, 16, 20, 63, 96–98, 101, 113, 129
myriad, 136, 151

present, 85, 92, 100, 148, 174, 180
presentation, 80
press, 52–54
pressure, 7, 41, 61, 63, 66, 81, 86, 88, 93, 95, 106, 107, 122, 129
price, 106, 108
pride, 90, 159
principle, 38, 49, 143
privilege, 141
probability, 156
problem, 39, 85, 112, 121
process, 4, 22, 27, 30–33, 36–38, 41, 42, 44, 46, 47, 58, 73, 74, 85, 99, 100, 104, 110, 111, 116, 117, 119, 122, 144, 147, 150–152, 155, 163, 164, 172, 173
prodigy, 10
producer, 41, 126, 165
product, 37, 47, 49, 134, 164
production, 20, 39, 100, 108, 117, 150, 163, 165, 175
productivity, 72
professional, 80, 92, 93, 95, 107, 111, 121, 164
professionalism, 94
proficiency, 14
profile, 106, 123
progression, 14, 117, 118, 154
project, 16, 36, 41, 110, 116, 144
prominence, 53
promise, 4, 23
promotion, 49, 51, 52, 108
proposal, 100
prospect, 172
prowess, 3, 7, 39, 81, 113, 116, 175
proximity, 79
psyche, 125
psychology, 82

public, 52, 86, 93, 106, 126, 129, 168
pulse, 136
purpose, 82, 152, 172
pursuit, 17, 20, 23, 101, 107, 109

quality, 88, 100, 117, 121, 166
quest, 112, 129, 162
question, 23

radio, 52–54, 123
range, 13, 76
rate, 132, 133
reach, 54, 56, 82, 88, 89, 138, 151
reaction, 4
reaffirmation, 174
reality, 4, 40, 81, 89, 93, 97, 108, 126, 129, 161
realization, 143, 159
realm, 30, 77, 112, 118, 145, 175
reasoning, 100
reception, 51, 110, 122, 124
recipe, 25
recognition, 9, 10, 85, 94, 108
recollection, 158
reconfiguration, 73
reconnection, 170
record, 45, 93, 123
recording, 27, 36–38, 41, 42, 46, 47, 100, 110, 111, 120–122, 144, 150, 152, 163
reevaluation, 93
refinement, 36, 37
refining, 36, 38, 150
reflection, 2, 12, 23, 62, 93, 111, 131, 150, 172
regimen, 65
regret, 152
rehearsal, 70, 72, 74, 81, 87
relatability, 116

Index

relation, 74
relationship, 81, 91, 97, 117
release, 110, 111, 117, 122, 153
reminder, 40, 66, 70, 94, 96, 98, 103, 108, 136, 143, 148, 153, 157, 159, 160, 168, 174, 179
repertoire, 66, 134, 137
replication, 6
representation, 120
reputation, 151
resilience, 22, 27, 41, 56, 62, 64, 65, 84, 93, 96, 103, 111, 131, 144, 150, 152, 159, 166
resolution, 100, 101, 117, 128
resolve, 69, 100
resonance, 116, 137, 155
resourcefulness, 62
respect, 27, 69, 100, 128, 148, 169
response, 39, 44, 48
responsibility, 93, 108, 141, 152, 167
rest, 66
result, 27, 54, 68, 74, 104, 119
rethinking, 80
retreat, 154
return, 131, 152, 174
reunion, 160, 168, 170, 172–174
review, 51
revitalization, 171
revolution, 89
rhythm, 10, 12, 13, 15, 20, 23, 70, 113, 126
richness, 114
ride, 41, 45, 151
riff, 27, 68, 70
right, 8, 25, 169
ripple, 51, 142
rise, 15, 53–55, 61, 107, 141, 166, 167, 175, 179

risk, 18, 39
ritual, 66, 148
road, 61–63, 65–67, 96, 98, 158, 160
roadside, 66, 158
roar, 4, 160
rock, 11, 15, 18, 46, 100, 104, 109, 112, 113, 123, 127, 128
rockstar, 94–97, 107
role, 2, 6, 8, 9, 11, 13, 14, 20, 22, 25, 32, 51, 52, 67, 89, 93, 116, 144, 158, 165
rollercoaster, 40, 45, 98, 151
room, 1, 41, 66, 108, 152
rush, 62, 63, 94

s, 1–18, 20–27, 39, 41, 42, 44, 53, 56, 57, 62–67, 72, 73, 78, 79, 81–86, 88–94, 97, 98, 100, 103, 107–113, 115–120, 122–126, 130, 131, 135–138, 140–143, 149, 151, 152, 154–156, 159, 160, 164–168, 174
sadness, 11, 98
safety, 66
sanctuary, 154
saying, 24, 155, 159
scale, 19, 61, 81, 94, 141
scenario, 95
scene, 12, 19, 47, 54, 57, 133, 136, 151, 174
schedule, 17, 66, 72, 97, 152
scheduling, 85
school, 3, 11, 13–17
science, 76
scrutiny, 106, 129
sculpture, 91
sea, 4

search, 119
section, 4, 8, 25, 33, 36, 38, 42, 44, 49, 63, 77, 89, 96, 109, 110, 118, 122, 136, 141, 151, 166, 168, 170, 175
selection, 77, 85
self, 65, 93, 107, 109, 130, 131, 152, 166, 167, 175
sensation, 55
sense, 13, 19, 26, 27, 44, 65, 70, 82, 83, 85, 87, 90, 91, 93, 117, 126, 131, 135, 142, 144, 150–152, 154, 155, 159, 166, 167, 172
sentiment, 141
separation, 64, 173
sequence, 15
serendipity, 25
series, 25, 55, 91, 106, 123, 148, 149, 155, 165, 171, 173
session, 24, 26, 27, 41, 46, 66, 70, 100, 150, 158
set, 1, 2, 10, 12, 15, 19, 23, 25, 32, 39, 49, 57, 61, 66, 69, 80, 106, 120, 121, 124, 143, 161, 169
setback, 41
setlist, 74–76, 159, 160, 179
setting, 10, 15, 70, 84
setup, 41
shadow, 7
shape, 37, 49, 91, 98, 124, 150
share, 23, 32, 48, 50, 54, 61, 65, 67, 83, 86, 87, 90, 98, 159, 162
shift, 61, 80, 83, 127
shout, 79
show, 55, 64, 66, 73, 74, 79, 158
showcase, 3, 9, 16, 44, 114, 119, 162
side, 62, 94, 114, 115

sight, 69, 73
signature, 3, 20–22, 123, 128, 154, 165
significance, 49, 143, 158, 159, 175, 177
Simone, 5
single, 11, 27, 41, 44, 46, 49, 51, 68, 70, 112, 121, 125, 126
situation, 158
size, 81
skepticism, 168
skill, 2, 10, 36, 47
sky, 122
smell, 23
snowball, 48
socializing, 93, 94
society, 143, 167
software, 41
solace, 17, 63, 98, 101, 131
solidarity, 84
solo, 16, 109, 114–116, 124, 126, 152, 162, 164, 166, 171
solution, 73
song, 2, 3, 26, 27, 31, 38, 39, 41, 53, 55, 77, 78, 104, 110–112, 125, 126, 150, 154, 157, 160, 179, 180
songwriting, 2, 3, 14, 15, 27, 30, 32, 33, 35, 36, 46, 68, 70, 111, 116–118, 130, 147, 150, 152, 154, 155, 164
sophomore, 122
sorrow, 159
soul, 23, 137, 160
sound, 1, 3–6, 8–10, 12, 13, 15, 20–27, 32, 34, 38–42, 44–47, 49, 51, 57, 61, 69, 72, 73, 79–81, 84, 99, 100, 104, 109–112, 115–123,

Index

127–129, 135, 136, 144, 147, 150, 152, 154, 162, 165, 167, 168, 171, 173, 175
soundscape, 112
soundtrack, 161
source, 33, 67, 122, 138
space, 70, 79, 174, 177
span, 11
spark, 4, 36, 70, 158, 168, 170
specific, 160
spectacle, 74, 80, 84, 156
spectatorship, 159
spectrum, 109
speculation, 168, 170, 172
speed, 62
spirit, 24, 28, 46, 63, 69, 79, 83, 84, 87, 117, 137, 148, 150, 152, 158, 170, 177, 180
spontaneity, 30, 63, 70
spot, 120
spotlight, 94, 131, 164, 165, 174
spring, 8
stadium, 81, 104, 179
stage, 2–4, 10, 12, 15, 23, 25, 26, 37, 42, 44, 47, 49, 55, 66, 67, 72–74, 79–81, 104, 120, 149, 151, 156, 159, 160, 180
standard, 57
standout, 27, 123
staple, 14, 55, 117, 154
star, 1, 2, 4, 141
stardom, 2, 49, 129, 131, 141, 143, 151, 152
state, 164
status, 53, 55, 104
step, 2, 12, 13, 41, 145, 149
stone, 10

stop, 62, 65
storm, 49, 123
storming, 25, 26
story, 1, 4, 10, 25, 63, 67, 84, 91, 103, 106, 108, 138, 143, 150, 158, 179
storytelling, 1, 12, 14, 52, 73, 74, 155, 159
strain, 64, 94, 108
street, 66, 122
strength, 28, 122
stress, 65, 107, 130
stretch, 66
structure, 18, 20, 29, 117, 126, 149, 154, 164, 175
struggle, 53, 112, 159
strum, 11
strumming, 3, 13, 70
studio, 37, 40–42, 44, 100, 104, 120, 121, 173
study, 14, 34
style, 3, 5, 9, 12, 13, 24, 30, 110, 112, 128, 135, 176
substance, 164
success, 25, 28, 33, 49, 54, 55, 57, 64, 68, 82, 84, 86, 89, 92–94, 96, 101, 106–108, 110, 111, 122–125, 133, 144, 151–153, 164, 165
sum, 24, 30, 144, 162
summary, 22, 28
superficiality, 143
support, 4, 49, 65, 67, 98, 131, 144, 157, 166
surface, 92
surprise, 4, 157
surrounding, 47, 73, 89, 91, 93, 155, 156
sustainability, 108

sword, 51, 62, 65, 94, 99, 101
symbol, 57
symphony, 70
sync, 160
synchronization, 81
syncopation, 113
synergy, 12, 24, 26, 27, 30, 53, 62, 68, 70, 74, 119, 120, 126, 150, 162
synth, 110, 112
system, 41, 85, 100, 117

table, 24, 26, 41, 46, 115, 173
take, 2, 4, 35, 37, 41, 53, 66, 111, 113, 118, 129
talent, 1–4, 7–10, 12, 14, 47, 49, 79, 116
talk, 56
tapestry, 2, 5, 10, 15, 18, 20, 26, 62, 67, 77, 89, 91, 97, 109, 118, 122, 147, 153, 168, 174
task, 7, 36
tattoo, 90
teacher, 11
teamwork, 64, 67
technique, 11, 117, 122
technology, 32, 44, 55, 56, 81, 113, 156
television, 8, 168
tempo, 73
temptation, 92, 93
tender, 3, 8, 12
tension, 62, 68, 84, 100, 117, 120, 128, 173
term, 96
territory, 39, 128
testament, 2, 10, 12, 22, 24, 33, 38, 41, 44, 47, 51, 69, 81, 91, 96, 98, 100, 105, 106, 111, 112, 114, 116, 120, 124, 136, 138, 148, 151, 159, 160, 166, 168, 174, 177, 179
testing, 34
texture, 117
theatricality, 1
theory, 9–11, 14, 15, 17, 44, 82, 109, 117, 166, 175
thing, 25
thought, 39, 66
thread, 77
thrill, 12, 62, 65, 67, 90, 94, 129, 158
thrive, 26, 94, 168
ticket, 156
ticketing, 85
tier, 55
tightrope, 94, 129
time, 16, 25, 32, 55, 67, 83, 85, 86, 97, 108, 113, 123, 126, 145, 158–160, 164, 170, 172, 174, 177
timelessness, 168
timing, 74, 81, 85
today, 4, 82
toll, 66, 86, 93, 101, 108, 129, 152, 174
tone, 154
tool, 49, 52, 55, 82, 86, 176
toolkit, 113
topic, 93
torch, 141
tour, 44, 55, 64–66, 73, 98, 104, 123, 148, 151, 153, 156, 158–160, 166, 170, 172, 174
touring, 61–67, 96–98, 101, 108, 152

Index

town, 1, 56
track, 41, 46, 68, 100, 110–113, 122, 126, 137, 150
traction, 82
tradition, 7, 8, 10
training, 14, 15
trajectory, 122, 149
tranquility, 9
transformation, 6, 81, 140, 164
transition, 42, 61, 80, 81, 83, 166
transparency, 69
travel, 62–64, 96, 108
treasure, 159
trend, 134
trepidation, 15, 173
tribute, 160, 180
trick, 14
trio, 23, 24
triumph, 159
trolling, 88
trove, 159
trust, 27, 35, 49, 69
Tuckman, 25
turbulence, 96
turmoil, 92, 101
turning, 11, 12, 67
tutelage, 9
twist, 25

ukulele, 11
understanding, 3, 10, 26, 62, 74, 76, 79, 108, 117, 128, 137, 141, 148
union, 25
unit, 27, 33, 65
unity, 27, 33, 65, 67, 135, 144, 150, 151
universe, 1, 23, 25
unmet, 98

unpredictability, 62, 64
up, 8, 20, 23, 70, 74, 80, 122
urge, 12, 124
use, 5, 88, 101, 103, 117, 138

validation, 9
value, 69, 90, 145
variable, 30
variety, 11, 168
vehicle, 141
venture, 39
venue, 63, 64, 81, 85, 156, 158, 174
versatility, 6, 10, 46, 110, 114, 116, 128, 152, 165, 171
version, 111
viability, 119
victory, 10
video, 80
vigor, 131
vinyl, 90
violin, 10
visibility, 111, 141
vision, 26, 27, 44, 62, 72, 91, 110–112, 118–120, 125, 128, 140, 143, 162, 163, 169, 172
visual, 55, 72–74, 80, 156, 168
vocabulary, 13
vocal, 3, 5
vocalist, 12, 68
voice, 1, 3, 13, 14, 18, 19, 34, 160
vulnerability, 82, 103, 145, 155, 161, 164, 165

warmth, 154
wave, 54, 57, 179
way, 2, 6, 8, 12, 23, 34, 47, 54, 87, 108, 124, 129, 138, 153, 160, 161, 170

wealth, 8, 18, 94
web, 92
weight, 31, 106, 148, 155, 158–160, 170
well, 7, 13, 54, 72, 84, 86, 95, 98, 107, 115, 119, 122, 123, 126, 130, 152
whirlwind, 24, 61, 65, 92, 96
Whitney Houston, 3
whole, 24, 162, 166
willingness, 21, 39, 40, 62, 110, 111, 113, 150, 152, 169, 170
Wilson, 7
wisdom, 145
word, 49–51, 82
work, 3, 5, 6, 17, 18, 39, 41, 44, 49, 91, 94, 96, 106, 109, 111, 112, 116, 124, 159
workflow, 32
working, 12, 16, 41, 144, 165
world, 1–4, 8–12, 23, 25, 32, 38, 42, 54, 55, 67, 72, 84, 86, 92, 94, 96, 98–100, 111, 119, 124, 136–138, 151, 154, 159, 164, 167, 168
writing, 27, 32, 36, 38

yoga, 65
youth, 167

zeitgeist, 55, 109, 168
zone, 40